Lecture Notes in Artificial Intelligence　　13418

Subseries of Lecture Notes in Computer Science

More information about this subseries at https://link.springer.com/bookseries/1244

Fabio Cuzzolin · Kevin Cannons ·
Vincenzo Lomonaco (Eds.)

Continual Semi-Supervised Learning

First International Workshop, CSSL 2021
Virtual Event, August 19–20, 2021
Revised Selected Papers

 Springer

Editors
Fabio Cuzzolin🆔
Oxford Brookes University
Oxford, UK

Kevin Cannons
Huawei Technologies Canada Co., Ltd.
Burnaby, BC, Canada

Vincenzo Lomonaco🆔
University of Pisa
Pisa, Italy

ISSN 0302-9743   ISSN 1611-3349 (electronic)
Lecture Notes in Artificial Intelligence
ISBN 978-3-031-17586-2   ISBN 978-3-031-17587-9 (eBook)
https://doi.org/10.1007/978-3-031-17587-9

LNCS Sublibrary: SL7 – Artificial Intelligence

This Springer imprint is published by the registered company Springer Nature Switzerland AG
The registered company address is: Gewerbestrasse 11, 6330 Cham, Switzerland

Preface

Whereas continual learning has recently attracted much attention in the machine learning community, the focus has been mainly on preventing the model updated in the light of new data from 'catastrophically forgetting' its initial knowledge and abilities. This, however, is in stark contrast with common real-world situations in which an initial model is trained using limited data, only to be later deployed without any additional supervision. In these scenarios the goal is for the model to be incrementally updated using the new (unlabelled) data, in order to adapt to a target domain continually shifting over time.

These situations can be modelled by an original *continual semi-supervised learning* (CSSL) paradigm. There, an initial training batch of data-points annotated with ground truth (class labels for classification problems, or vectors of target values for regression ones) is available and can be used to train an initial model. Then, however, the model is incrementally updated by exploiting the information provided by a stream of unlabelled data points, each of which is generated by a data generating process (modelled, as typically assumed, by a probability distribution) which varies with time. No artificial subdivision into 'tasks' is assumed, as the data-generating distribution may arbitrarily vary over time.

The aim of the First International Workshop on Continual Semi-Supervised Learning (CSSL @ IJCAI 2021)[1] was to formalise this new learning paradigm and to introduce it to the wider machine learning community, in order to mobilise effort in this direction. As part of the workshop we also presented the first two benchmark datasets for this problem, derived from important computer vision scenarios, and proposed the first Continual Semi-Supervised Learning Challenges to the research community.

The workshop encouraged the submission of papers on continual learning in its broader sense, covering topics such as: the suitability of existing datasets for continual learning; new benchmark datasets explicitly designed for continual learning; protocols for training and testing in different continual learning settings; metrics for assessing continual learning methods; traditional task-based continual learning; the relation between continual learning and model adaptation; the distinction between the learning of new classes and the learning from new instances; real-world applications of continual learning; catastrophic forgetting and possible mitigation strategies; applications of transfer learning, multi-task and meta-learning to continual learning; continual supervised, semi-supervised and unsupervised learning; lifelong learning; few-shot learning; and continual reinforcement and inverse reinforcement learning.

The aim was to foster the debate around all aspects of continual learning, especially those which are the subject of ongoing frontier research. As part of the event, we invited both paper track contributions on the above-mentioned topics as well as submissions of entries to two challenges specifically designed to test CSSL approaches. To this purpose, two new benchmarks, a Continual Activity Recognition (CAR) dataset[2] and a Continual

---

[1] https://sites.google.com/view/sscl-workshop-ijcai-2021/.

[2] https://github.com/salmank255/IJCAI-2021-Continual-Activity-Recognition-Challenge.

Crowd Counting (CCC) dataset, were specifically designed to assess continual semi-supervised learning on two important computer vision tasks: activity recognition and crowd counting.

Papers submitted to the workshop were asked to follow the standard IJCAI 2021 template (6 pages plus 1 for the references). Paper submission took place through Easy-Chair[3]. Authors were allowed to submit a supplementary material document with details on their implementation. However, reviewers were not required to consult this additional material when assessing the submission. A double-blind review process was followed. Authors were asked not include any identifying information (names, affiliations, etc.) or links and self-references that could reveal their identities. Each submission received three reviews from members of the Program Committee, which assessed it based on relevance, novelty and potential for impact. No rebuttal stage was introduced. The authors of the accepted papers were asked to guarantee their presence at the workshop, with at least one author for each accepted paper registering for the conference. The workshop allowed for the presentation during the workshop of results published elsewhere, but these papers were not considered for or included in these published proceedings.

The paper submission deadline was initially set to June 15, 2021, but was later extended to July 2, 2021. Authors were notified of the result on July 19, 2021, and asked to submit a camera-ready version of their paper by July 31. A total of 14 papers were submitted, of which one was withdrawn and one rejected, for an acceptance rate of 86% of papers presented at the workshop, while the rate of acceptance for papers intended for the published proceedings is 69%, 9 papers. The 20 members of the Program Committee were assigned on average two papers to review each.

The workshop issued a Best Paper Award to the author(s) of the best accepted paper, as judged by the Organising Committee based on the reviews assigned by PC members, as well as a Best Student Paper Award, selected in the same way and a Prize to be awarded to the winners of each of the Challenges. The Best Paper Award was assigned to "SPeCiaL: Self-Supervised Pretraining for Continual Learning", by Lucas Caccia and Joelle Pineau. The Best Student Paper Award was secured by "Hypernetworks for Continual Semi-Supervised Learning", by Dhanajit Brahma, Vinay Kumar Verma and Piyush Rai.

The workshop took place on August 19–20, 2021, as a full-day event split into two 4-hour halves. The event was articulated into:

- A brief introduction by the organisers.
- A presentation of the new benchmark datasets and associated challenges.
- Invited talks by top researchers in the area, with brief Q&A session after each invited talk.
- Oral presentations for the Best Paper and the Best Student Paper.
- Spotlight talks for the winners of the Challenges.
- Two poster sessions (a morning session and an afternoon session) for all other accepted papers.
- A discussion panel on the future of continual learning from long streams of unlabelled data.

---

[3] https://easychair.org/my/conference?conf=csslijcai2021.

There were four invited talks, 30 minutes per talk, given by top researchers in the field: Razvan Pascanu (Deepmind), Tinne Tuytelaars (KU Leuven), Chelsea Finn (Stanford) and Bing Liu (University of Illinois at Chicago). Titles and abstracts for the invited talks are provided at the end of the front matter.

With respect to the paper topics in these proceedings, several focus on the central workshop theme of learning from unlabelled data. "SPeCiaL: Self-Supervised Pretraining for Continual Learning" borrowed ideas from representation and meta-learning to pretrain a neural network from unlabelled data such that it is more amenable to continual learning tasks. Other approaches considered clustering-based algorithms to address the lack of labels. For instance "Unsupervised Continual Learning via Self-Adaptive Deep Clustering Approach" proposed a self-evolving deep clustering network, which can adapt rapidly to changing data distributions found in the deployment environment. On the other hand, "Unsupervised Continual Learning Via Pseudo Labels" leveraged K-means clustering to assign pseudo labels to unlabelled data, from which a class incremental learner was trained. These pseudo labels were shown to be effective when used within the context of several supervised continual learning algorithms.

The challenge of catastrophic forgetting was also addressed by several papers, with particular emphasis on replay-based approaches. "A Benchmark and Empirical Analysis for Replay Strategies in Continual Learning" completed a rigorous analysis of eight established replay strategies used in continual learning and evaluated them using efficiency, accuracy, and scalability-based metrics. The issue of minimizing the size of the replay buffer was considered in "Distilled Replay: Overcoming Forgetting through Synthetic Samples", where a dataset distillation approach was used to identify highly informative samples.

Additional themes were considered by many of the other contributions to the workshop. The artificial subdivision of data into 'tasks' was addressed in "Self-Supervised Novelty Detection for Continual Learning: A Gradient-based Approach Boosted by Binary Classification", where the detection of out of distribution data was assumed to correspond to the task boundaries. Further, the use of continual learning within the robotics domain was explored in "Transfer and Continual Supervised Learning for Robotic Grasping through Grasping Features". This paper showed that higher-level grasping features are more amenable to transfer/continual learning tasks than purely visual features. Finally, "Evaluating Continual Learning Algorithms by Generating 3D Virtual Environments" introduced a 3D simulation tool that provides a highly customizable and controllable environment for continual learning experiments. Simulation scenarios can be created that allow different objects to move along variable routes within an environment. Thus, this simulator can be used to create more natural continual learning datasets than the somewhat artificial ones that are often used and derived from standard computer vision literature.

April 2022

Fabio Cuzzolin
Kevin Cannons
Vincenzo Lomonaco

Organization

General Chair

Fabio Cuzzolin   Oxford Brookes University, UK

Program Committee Chairs

Kevin Cannons   Huawei Technologies, Canada
Vincenzo Lomonaco   University of Pisa, Italy

Steering Committee

Mohammad Asiful Hossain Huawei Technologies, Canada
Salman Khan   Oxford Brookes University, UK
Irina Rish   University of Montreal and MILA, Canada
Ajmal Shahbaz   Oxford Brookes University, UK

Program Committee

Aishwarya Balwani   Georgia Institute of Technology, USA
Tudor Berariu   University Politehnica of Bucharest, Romania
Laurent Charlin   Columbia University, USA
Nikhil Churamani   University of Cambridge, UK
Andrea Cossu   Scuola Normale Superiore, Pisa, Italy
Matthias De Lange   KU Leuven, Belgium
Yunhui Guo   UC Berkeley, USA
Naeemullah Khan   University of Oxford, UK
Umberto Michieli   University of Padua, Italy
Oleksiy Ostapenko   University of Montreal and MILA, Canada
Marcello Pelillo   University of Venice, Italy
Amanda Rios   University of Southern California, USA
Martha White   Indiana University Bloomington, USA

Invited Talks

Continual Learning: The Challenge

Razvan Pascanu

DeepMind, UK

In this talk I want to start by drawing attention to the definition of continual learning. In particular I want to emphasize one particular perspective that equates continual learning to solving the credit assignment problem, namely which weights get blamed for the observed error. This implies that a solution to continual learning has to lead to more computationally efficient learning and can impact even in the IID setting. The second half of the talk highlights a few interesting limitations or observations regarding not only continual learning but also the learning process in general. Namely I will briefly discuss whether the typical assumption made by regularization based methods of CL is realistic for the benchmarks we typically use. I will touch on the question of plasticity, arguing that the learning process does not only catastrophically forget, but might also lose plasticity as learning progresses and finally I will approach the question of representation learning and the role it might play in a continual learning system.

Continual and On-the-Job Learning

Bing Liu

University of Illinois at Chicago, USA

In the existing machine learning paradigm, once a model is deployed in an application, it is fixed and there is no more learning. However, many real-life environments such as those of cellphones, chatbots and self-driving cars are highly dynamic and full of unknowns. Such environments demand continuous learning and model adaptation and improvement during applications and on device. We call this on-the-job learning. We humans learn about 70% of our knowledge on the job or while working and only about 10% through formal education. AI systems should have the same on-the-job learning capability to make them autonomous. It is very costly and inefficient for them to rely solely on manually labeled data and offline training to deal with the constantly changing and open world. In this talk, I will discuss this problem and some of our recent work.

Continual Learning: Some Reflections

Tinne Tuytelaars

KU Leuven, Belgium

In this talk, I reflect on the recent progress in the field of deep continual learning.

In se, continual learning promises to address several of the core limitations of today's deep learning machinery: its lack of robustness and limited generalization capabilities, its need for large-scale curated and representative datasets, its tendency to overfit to any such dataset, its large carbon footprint due to regular retraining of models when new data becomes available, etc. While interesting new approaches have been proposed over the years, that deepen our insights in the learning process, there's no satisfactory solution yet to date. Simply storing a buffer with a set of exemplars for replay, often seems the most practical solution and a remarkably strong baseline. Moving beyond this local optimum, I think it's important we scale up to real world settings and problems. Maybe not having access to any old data is too strict. Yet so is the assumption of mutually exclusive tasks, common in the now dominant class-incremental setting. Instead, a domain-incremental learning setting, where the global task that needs to be solved remains the same, is arguably a more realistic and relevant setting. Few methods to date have been designed specifically for this setting. Further, we should pay more attention to other vision problems beyond classification, such as detection or segmentation. Finally, we should move beyond task sequences, aiming for methods that can cope with streaming data. Working with real data, new and so far under-investigated problems pop up, such as dealing with class imbalances and rare events, leveraging large pretrained models or exploiting domain knowledge. The challenge we organize in the context of the SSLAD workshop at ICCV, focusing on an autonomous driving application, is a good case in point.

At the same time, I advocate we should not give up research on the academic setups consisting of splits of datasets and the like. These provide us with a controlled setting, where the data distribution shifts are known and their effect can be analyzed in depth. We're still in dire need of a better understanding of the learning dynamics, if we want to find out how to counter forgetting and drift.

Contents

International Workshop on Continual Semi-Supervised Learning: Introduction, Benchmarks and Baselines

Ajmal Shahbaz[1(✉)], Salman Khan[1], Mohammad Asiful Hossain[2],
Vincenzo Lomonaco[3], Kevin Cannons[2], Zhan Xu[2], and Fabio Cuzzolin[1]

[1] Oxford Brookes University, Oxford, UK
{ashahbaz,salmankhan,fabio.cuzzolin}@brookes.ac.uk
[2] Huawei Technologies, Vancouver, Canada
{mohammad.asiful.hossain,kevin.cannons,zhan.xu}@huawei.com
[3] University of Pisa, Pisa, Italy
vincenzo.lomonaco@unipi.it

Abstract. The aim of this paper is to formalise a new continual semi-supervised learning (CSSL) paradigm, proposed to the attention of the machine learning community via the IJCAI 2021 International Workshop on Continual Semi-Supervised Learning (CSSL@IJCAI) (https://sites.google.com/view/sscl-workshop-ijcai-2021/), with the aim of raising the field's awareness about this problem and mobilising its effort in this direction. After a formal definition of continual semi-supervised learning and the appropriate training and testing protocols, the paper introduces two new benchmarks specifically designed to assess CSSL on two important computer vision tasks: activity recognition and crowd counting. We describe the Continual Activity Recognition (CAR) and Continual Crowd Counting (CCC) challenges built upon those benchmarks, the baseline models proposed for the challenges, and describe a simple CSSL baseline which consists in applying batch self-training in temporal sessions, for a limited number of rounds. The results show that learning from unlabelled data streams is extremely challenging, and stimulate the search for methods that can encode the dynamics of the data stream.

Keywords: Continual learning · Semi-supervised learning · Artificial intelligence

1 Introduction

Whereas the continual learning problem has been recently the object of much attention in the machine learning community, the latter has mainly studied from the point of view of class-incremental learning [23], in particular with a focus on preventing the model updated in the light of new data from 'catastrophic forgetting' its initial, useful knowledge and abilities. A typical example is that of

F. Cuzzolin et al. (Eds.): CSSL 2021, LNAI 13418, pp. 1–14, 2022.
https://doi.org/10.1007/978-3-031-17587-9_1

an object detector which needs to be extended to include classes not originally in its list (e.g., 'donkey') while retaining its ability to correctly detect, say, a 'horse'. The hidden assumption there is that we are quite satisfied with the model we have, and we merely wish to extend its capabilities to new settings and classes [18].

This way of posing the continual learning problem, however, is in rather stark contrast with widespread real-world situations in which an initial model is trained using limited data, only for it to then be deployed without any additional supervision. Think of a detector used for traffic monitoring on a busy street. Even after having been trained extensively on the many available public datasets, experience shows that its performance in its target setting will likely be less than optimal. In this scenario, the objective is for the model to be incrementally updated using the new (unlabelled) data, in order to adapt to its new target domain.

In such settings the goal is quite the opposite to that of the classical scenario described above: the initial model is usually rather poor and not a good match for the target domain. To complicate things further, the target domain itself may change over time, both periodically (think of night/day cycles) and in asynchronous, discrete steps (e.g., when a new bank opens within the camera's field of view, or a new building is erected with a new entrance) [2].

In this paper we formalise this problem as one of *continual semi-supervised learning*, in which an initial training batch of labelled data points is available and can be used to train an initial model, but then the model is incrementally updated exploiting the information provided by a time series of unlabelled data points, each of which is generated by a data generating process (modelled by a probability distribution) which *varies with time*. We do not assume any artificial subdivision into 'tasks', but allow the data generating distribution to be an arbitrary function of time.

While batch semi-supervised learning (SSL) has seen renewed interest in recent times, thanks to relevant work in the rising field of unsupervised domain adaptation [22] and various approaches based on classical SSL self-training [5,19], continual SSL is still a rather unexplored field. The reason is that, while in the supervised case it is clear what information the streaming data points carry, in the semi-supervised case it is far from obvious what relevant information carried by the streaming instance should drive model update.

1.1 Contributions

With this paper we wish to contribute:

1. A formal definition of the continual semi-supervised learning problem, and the associated training and testing protocols, as a basis for future work in this area.
2. The first two benchmark datasets for the validation of semi-supervised continual learning approaches, one for classification (continual activity recognition, CAR) and one for regression (continual crowd counting, CCC), which we propose as the foundations of the first challenges in this domain.

3. Results produced by a simple strategy in which self-training is applied in sessions to competitive baseline models on both benchmarks, as the foundations for the above challenges.

Our results confirm that continual semi-supervised learning is a very challenging task, and that strategies that fail to model the dynamics of the unlabelled data stream have limited performance potential.

1.2 Paper Outline

The structure of the paper is as follows. First we discuss some relevant related work in continual supervised learning and semi-supervised learning (Sect. 2). We then introduce the principle and framework of our continual semi-supervised learning approach (Sect. 3), in particular the relevant training and testing protocols. In Sect. 4 we introduce our new benchmark datasets, while in Sect. 5 we illustrate the IJCAI 2021 challenges based upon those datasets and the activity detection and crowd counting approaches we adopted as baselines, together with our simple self-training strategy for tackling the challenge. In Sect. 6 we illustrate our baseline results for the two challenges. Section 7 concludes.

2   Related Work

2.1   Continual Supervised Learning

Continual learning refers to the ability of a system to keep learning from new data throughout its lifetime, even beyond an initial training stage, allowing the system to adapt to new, ever evolving situations ('domain adaptation'). Continual learning can be supervised, when new annotation is provided even after the system is deployed, or unsupervised/semi-supervised if, after training on an initial batch of annotated data-points (e.g., videos with an attached 'event' label, or images with superimposed manually drawn skeletons of the humans in the scene), the data subsequently captured cannot be annotated. In supervised continual learning, the focus of the community has been so far on the issue of avoiding 'catastrophic forgetting', i.e., models that forget their previous abilities and they keep being updated in the light of new data.

   Current continual learning methods can be categorised into three major families based on how the information of previous data are stored and used. *Prior-focused* methods [11] use a penalty term to regularise the parameters rather than a hard constraint. *Parameter isolation* methods [17] dedicate different parameters for different tasks to prevent interference. Finally, *replay-based* approaches store the examples' information in a 'replay buffer' or a generative model, which is used for rehearsal/retraining or to provide constraints on the current learning step [1].

2.2   Continual Learning as Constrained Optimisation

In particular, in a recent paper [1], continual supervised learning is formulated in terms of the following optimization problem, for any time instant t: $\theta_t = \arg\min_\theta l(f(x_t|\theta), y_t)$, subject to the constraints that $l(f(x_\tau|\theta), y_\tau) \leq l(f(x_\tau|\theta_{t-1}), y_\tau)$, $\forall \tau = 1, \ldots, t-1$, where y_τ is the true label of instance x_τ, and θ_t is the version of the model at time t. The loss function $l(y', y)$ assesses how well the predicted label y' matches the actual label y.

The aim of supervised continual learning as formulated above is to incrementally learn a model able to best adapt to each new data-point, while ensuring that the loss of the new model on the past observed data-points is no greater than the loss of the previous version of the model there. Note that not all cost functions in model learning correspond to the average of some loss over the training examples. A (hidden) assumption in [1] is, therefore, that learning happens by minimising this average ('empirical loss').

The problem is designed to avoid catastrophic forgetting at instance (rather than class) level, as new models are required to have a non-increasing loss on the instances seen up to then.

2.3   Unsupervised Domain Adaptation

Batch semi-supervised learning (SSL) has seen renewed interest in recent times, thanks to relevant work in the rising field of *unsupervised domain adaptation*, where the dominant trend is based on adversarial approaches to reduce the discrepancy between source and target domain features [8,22]. Many deep self-training approaches have been proposed, inspired by the classical SSL self-training algorithm, which alternate between generating pseudo-labels for the unlabelled data-points and re-training a deep classifier (including the intermediate layers producing the feature embeddings) [6]. Despite all this, continual semi-supervised learning remains a rather unexplored field and [14].

3   Continual Semi-Supervised Learning

We begin by formalising the continual semi-supervised learning problem, and by defining the appropriate training and testing protocols for this new learning setting.

3.1   Learning

The *continual semi-supervised learning* problem can be formulated as follows.

Given an initial batch of supervised training examples,

$$\mathcal{T}_0 = \{(x^j, y^j), j = 1, \ldots, N\},$$

and a stream of unsupervised examples,

$$\mathcal{T}_t = \{x_1, \ldots, x_t, \ldots\},$$

we wish to learn a model $f(x|\theta)$ mapping instances $x \in \mathcal{X}$ to target values $y \in \mathcal{Y}$, depending on a vector $\theta \in \Theta$ of parameters.

When $\mathcal{Y}$ is discrete (i.e., a list of labels) the problem is one of continual semi-supervised *classification*; when $\mathcal{Y}$ is continuous we talk about continual semi-supervised *regression*.

In both cases we wish the model to be updated incrementally as the string of unsupervised samples come in: namely, based on the current instance x_t at time t, model θ_{t-1} is mapped to a new model θ_t.

3.2 Testing

How should such a series of models be evaluated? In continual supervised learning (see e.g. [1]), a series of ground-truth target values is available and can be exploited to update the model. To avoid overfitting, the series of models outputted by a continual supervised learner, $f(x|\theta_1), \ldots, f(x|\theta_t), \ldots$ cannot be tested on the same data it was trained upon. Thus, basically all continual (supervised) learning papers set aside from the start a set of instances upon which the incremental models are tested (e.g., in the Core50 dataset the last three sessions are designated as test fold [16]).

In principle, however, as each model $f(x|\theta_t)$ is estimated at time t it should also be tested on data available at time t, possibly coming from a parallel (test) data stream. An idealised such scenario is one in which a person detector is continually trained on data coming from one surveillance camera, say in a shopping mall, and the resulting model is deployed (tested) in real time on all other cameras in the same mall.

In our continual semi-supervised setting, model update cannot make use of any ground truth target values. If the latter are somehow available, but not shown to the learner for training purposes, the performance of the learner can in fact be evaluated on the stream of true target values by testing at each time t model $f(x|\theta_t)$ on the data pair (x_t, y_t). A reasonable choice for a performance measure is the average loss of the series of models on the *contemporary* data pair:

$$\sum_{t=1,\ldots,T} l(f(x_t|\theta_t), y_t). \tag{1}$$

In our experiments a standard 0/1 loss, which translates into classical accuracy, is used for classification tasks.

4 Benchmark Datasets

To empirically validate CSSL approaches in a computer vision setting we created two benchmark datasets, one designed to test continual classification (CAR), and one for continual regression (CCC).

4.1   Continual Activity Recognition (CAR) Dataset

The MEVA Dataset. To allow the validation of continual semi-supervised learning approaches in a realistic classification task we created a new *continual activity recognition* (CAR) dataset derived from the very recently released MEVA (Multiview Extended Video with Activities) dataset [9].

MEVA is part of the EctEV (Activities in Extended Video) challenge[1]. As of December 2019, 328 h of ground-camera data and 4.2 h of Unmanned Arial Vehicle video had been released, broken down into 4304 video clips, each 5 min long. These videos were captured at 19 sites (e.g. School, Bus station, Hospital) of the Muscatatuck Urban Training Center (MUTC), using a team of over 100 actors performing in various scenarios. There are annotations for 22.1 h (266 five-minute-long video clips) of data. The original annotations are available on GitLab[2]. Each video frame is annotated in terms of 37 different activity classes relevant to video surveillance (e.g. *person_opens_facility_door*, *person_reads_document*, *vehicle_picks_up_person*). Each activity is annotated in terms of class labels and bounding boxes around the activity of interest. Whenever activities relate to objects or other persons (e.g., in *person_loads_vehicle* the person usually puts an object into the vehicle's trunk; in *person_talks_to_person* a number of people listen to the person speaking), these object(s) or people are also identified by a bounding box, to allow human-object interaction analyses.

The CAR Dataset. The original MEVA dataset comes with a number of issues, from our standpoint: (i) multiple activity classes can take place simultaneously, whereas in our formulation (at least for now) only one label can be emitted at any given time instant; (ii) the quality of the original annotation is uneven, with entire instances of activities missing. As our tests are about classification, we can neglect the bounding box information.

For these reasons we set about creating our own continual activity recognition (CAR) dataset by selecting 45 video clips from MEVA and generating from scratch a modified set of annotations spanning a reduced set of 8 activity classes (e.g. *person_enters_scene_through_structure*, *person_exits_vehicle*, *vehicle_starts*). Those 8 classes have been suitably selected from the original 37 to ensure that activity instances from different classes do not temporally overlap, so that we can assign a single label to each frame. Each instance of activity is annotated with the related start and end frame. Frames that do not contain any relevant activity label are assigned to a 'background' class. The goal is to classify the activity label of each input video frame.

For some MEVA sites, contiguous annotated videos exist with no gap between the end of the first video and the start of the second video. For some sites, 'almost' contiguous videos separated by short (5 or 15 min) gaps are available. Finally, videos from a same site separated by hours or days exist. Accordingly, our CAR benchmark is composed of 15 sequences, broken down into three groups:

---

[1] https://actev.nist.gov/.

[2] https://gitlab.kitware.com/meva/meva-data-repo/tree/master/annotation/DIVA-phase-2/MEVA/.

1. Five 15-minute-long sequences from sites G326, G331, G341, G420, and G638 formed by three original videos which are contiguous.
2. Five 15-minute-long sequences from sites G329, G341, G420, G421, G638 formed by three videos separated by a short gap (5–20 min).
3. Five 15-minute-long sequences from sites G420, G421, G424, G506, and G638 formed by three original videos separated by a long gap (hours or days).

Each of these three evaluation settings is intended to simulate a different mix of continuous and discrete domain dynamics.

The CAR dataset including annotation and scripts is available on GitHub[3].

4.2   The Continual Crowd Counting (CCC) Dataset

Crowd counting is the problem of, given a video frame, counting the number of people present in the frame. While intrinsically a classification problem, crowd counting can be posed as a regression problem by manually providing for each training frame a density map [3]. To date, crowd counting is mostly considered an image-based task, performed on single video frames. Few attempts have been made to extend the problem to the video domain [12,15,24].

To the best of our knowledge, continual crowd counting has never been posed as a problem, not even in the fully supervised context – thus, there are no standard benchmarks one can adopt in this domain. For this reason we set about assembling the first benchmark dataset for *continual crowd counting* (CCC). Our CCC dataset is composed by 3 sequences, taken from existing crowd counting datasets:

1. A single 2,000 frame sequence originally from the Mall dataset[4] [7].
2. A single 2,000-frame sequence originally from the UCSD dataset[5] [4].
3. A 750-frame sequence from the Fudan-ShanghaiTech (FDST) dataset[6], composed by 5 clips, 150 frames long, portraying a same scene [10].

The ground truth for the CCC sequences (in the form of a density map for each frame) was generated by us for all three datasets following a standard annotation protocol[7].

The CCC dataset complete with scripts for download and generating the baseline results is available on GitHub[8].

---

[3] https://github.com/salmank255/IJCAI-2021-Continual-Activity-Recognition-Challenge.
[4] https://www.kaggle.com/c/counting-people-in-a-mall.
[5] http://www.svcl.ucsd.edu/projects/peoplecnt/.
[6] https://drive.google.com/drive/folders/19c2X529VTNjl3YL1EYweBg60G70G2D-w.
[7] https://github.com/svishwa/crowdcount-mcnn.
[8] https://github.com/Ajmal70/IJCAI_2021_Continual_Crowd_Counting_Challenge.

5   Challenges

5.1   Protocols

CAR Challenge. From our problem definition (Sect. 3), once a model is fine-tuned on the supervised portion of a data stream it is then both incrementally updated using the unlabelled portion of the same data stream and tested there, using the provided ground truth. Incremental training and testing are supposed to happen independently for each sequence, as the aim is to simulate real-world scenarios in which a smart device with continual learning capability can only learn from its own data stream. However, as CAR sequences do not contain instances of all 9 activities, the initial supervised training is run there on the union of the supervised folds for each sequence.

Split. Each data stream (sequence) in our benchmark(s) is divided into a supervised fold (S), a validation fold (V) and a test fold (T), the last two unsupervised. Specifically, in CAR given a sequence the video frames from the first five minutes $(5 \times 60 \times 25 = 7{,}500$ samples) are selected to form the initial supervised training set S. The second clip (another 5 min) is provided as validation fold to tune the CSSL strategy. The remaining clip (5 min) is used as test fold for testing the performance of the (incrementally updated) classifier.

Evaluation. Performance is evaluated as the average performance of the incrementally updated classifier over the test fold for all the 15 sequences. More specifically, we evaluate the average accuracy (percentage of correctly classified frames) over the test folds of the 15 sequences. Remember that, however, in our setting each test frame is classified by the *current* model available at time t *for that specific sequence*. This distinguishes our evaluation setting from classical ones in which all samples at test time are processed by the same model, whose accuracy is then assessed.

CCC Challenge. Unlike the CAR challenge, in the crowd counting case (as this is a regression problem) each sequence is treated completely independently.

Split. For the CCC challenge we distinguish two cases. For the 2,000-frame sequences from either the UCSD or the Mall dataset, S is formed by the first 400 images, V by the following 800 images, and T by the remaining 800 images. For the 750-frame sequence from the FDST dataset, S is the set of the first 150 images, V the set of the following 300 images, and T the set of remaining 300 images.

Evaluation. For continual crowd counting, MAE (Mean Absolute Error) is adopted (as standard in the field) to measure performance. MAE is calculated using predicted and ground truth density maps in a regression setting.

5.2   Tasks

For our IJCAI challenge we therefore set four different validation experiments (*tasks*) (Fig. 1).

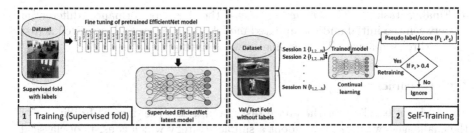

Fig. 1. Overall pipeline of our CAR baseline. 1) Firstly, a pre-trained EfficientNet model is fine-tuned over the supervised fold of the dataset (jointly over the 15 sequences). 2) The unlabeled validation and test folds are divided into subfolds. In each session video frames from each sub-fold are used in a self-training cycle in which a pseudo label P_L with prediction probability score P_s is generated for each frame, but only the pseudolabels with P_s above a fixed threshold (namely, 0.4) are considered as ground truth for retraining the model. Frames with lower P_s are ignored. The model updated by self-training in session n is used as initial model in session $n + 1$.

Table 1. Performance of the initial supervised model versus that of the incrementally updated models (separately on V and T or in combination), using three standard evaluation metrics. For each metric we report both class average (C) and weighted average (W).

Methods	Validation fold						Test fold					
	Precision		Recall		F1-Score		Precision		Recall		F1-score	
	C	W	C	W	C	W	C	W	C	W	C	W
$sup - ft - union$	**0.20**	**0.74**	**0.25**	0.68	**0.16**	0.70	**0.16**	**0.82**	**0.15**	0.77	**0.14**	0.79
$upd - V/upd - T$	0.18	0.73	0.19	**0.73**	0.14	**0.72**	0.14	0.81	**0.15**	**0.81**	**0.14**	**0.80**
$upd - V + T$	0.17	0.73	0.19	**0.73**	0.14	**0.72**	0.14	0.80	0.14	0.79	0.13	0.79

1. In the first task (*CAR-absolute*) the goal is to achieve the best average performance across all the (test folds of the) 15 sequences in the CAR dataset. The choice of the baseline action recognition model is left to the participants.
2. In the second task (*CAR-incremental*) the goal is to achieve the best performance differential between the model as updated through the chosen CSSL strategy and the original model fine-tuned over the supervised fold. We thus evaluate the difference between the average performance of the incrementally updated model on the test fold and the average performance of initial model, also on the test fold. The baseline recognition model is set by us (see Baselines).
3. Task *CCC-absolute* seeks the best average performance over the test fold of the 3 sequences of the CCC dataset. The choice of the baseline crowd counting model is left to the participants to encourage them to push its performance to the limit.

4. Finally, task *CCC-incremental* seeks the best performance differential between the initial and the updated model over the test fold, averaged across the three sequences. The baseline crowd counting model is set.

5.3   Baselines

To provide a baseline for the above tasks, and assess the degree of difficulty of the challenges, we decided to adopt a simple strategy which consists of classical (batch) semi-supervised self-training *performed in a series of sessions*, for both the activity and the crowd counting experiments. Baselines are provided regarding the initial action recognition model to be used in the CAR tests, the base crowd counter to be used in the CCC tests, and the semi-supervised incremental learning process itself.

Baseline Activity Recognition Model. The baseline model is the recent EfficientNet network (model EfficientNet-B5) [20], pre-trained on the large-scale ImageNet dataset over 1000 classes. For our tests we initialised the model using those weights and changed the number of classes to 9 activities (see Sect. 4). Detailed information about its implementation, along with pre-trained models, can be found on Github[9]. The model is easily downloadable using the Python command "pip" (*pip install efficientnet-pytorch*).

Table 2. Evaluation on the CCC validation (V) and test (T) folds for different experimental setups. Here $sup - ft$, $upd - V$, and $upd - V + T$ refer to the supervised model fine-tuned on S, the model incrementally updated via self-training in sessions on the validation fold V, and the model incrementally updated on the combined validation V and test T folds, respectively. The average test MAE is reported for each model.

	Validation fold V			Test fold T		
	$FDST$	$UCSD$	$MALL$	$FDST$	$UCSD$	$MALL$
$sup - ft$	**5.17**	**6.36**	**6.65**	9.59	8.34	13.56
$upd - V$	6.05	7.58	7.40	**8.00**	**7.45**	16.38
$upd - V + T$	8.32	8.28	9.36	9.16	8.93	**9.46**

Baseline Crowd Counter. For the baseline crowd counting model, we selected the Multi-Column Convolutional Neural Network (MCNN) [26], whose (unofficial) implementation is publicly available[10] and uses PyTorch. MCNN was considered state-of-the-art when released in 2016, but is still commonly used as a standard baseline in more recent works, due to its competitive performance on public datasets (e.g., [13,25]. MCNN made significant contributions to crowd

---

[9] https://github.com/lukemelas/EfficientNet-PyTorch.
[10] https://github.com/svishwa/crowdcount-mcnn.

counting by proposing a network architecture better-equipped to deal with differing head sizes due to image resolution, perspective effects, distances between the camera and the people within the scene, etc. In a nutshell, this robustness to scale was achieved via a network composed of three parallel CNN columns, each of which used filters with different receptive field sizes, allowing each column to specialize for a particular scale of human head.

Pre-trained MCNN models are available for both the ShanghaiTech A and the ShanghaiTech B datasets. For our tests, as well as the Challenge, we chose to adopt the ShanghaiTechB pre-trained model.

Baseline Incremental Learning Strategy. As mentioned, our baseline for incremental learning from unlabelled data stream is instead based on a *vanilla self-training* approach [21]. For each sequence, the unlabelled data stream (without distinction between validation and test folds) is partitioned into a number of sub-folds. Each sub-fold spans 1 min in the CAR challenges, so that each unlabelled sequence is split into 10 sub-folds. Sub-folds span 100 frames in the CCC challenges, so that the UCSD and MALL sequences comprise 16 sub-folds whereas the FDST sequence contains only 6 sub-folds.

Starting with the model initially fine-tuned on the supervised portion of the data stream, self-training is successively applied in a batch fashion in sessions, one session for each sub-fold, for a single epoch (as we noticed that using multiple epochs would lead to results degradation). Self-training requires to select a confidence threshold above which predictions are selected as pseudolabels. In our tests we set a confidence threshold of 0.4. The predictions generated by the model obtained after one round of self-training upon a sub-fold are stored as baseline predictions for the current sub-fold. The model updated after each self-training session is used as initial model for the following session.

6   Results

6.1   Results on Activity Recognition

Three types of experiments were performed to measure: (i) the performance of the baseline model after fine-tuning on the union of the supervised folds for the 15 CAR sequences ($sup - ft - union$), without any continual learning; (ii) the performance obtained by incrementally updating the model (in sessions) using the unlabelled validation ($upd - V$) or test ($upd - T$) data streams, considered separately; (iii) the performance of self-training over validation and training folds considered as a single contiguous data stream, again in a session-wise manner ($upd - V + T$).

The results are shown in Table 1. The standard classification evaluation metrics precision, recall, and F1-score were used for evaluation. For each evaluation metric we computed both the *class average* (obtained by computing the score for each class and taking the average without considering the number of training samples in each class, i.e., $F1_{class1} + F1_{class2} \cdots + F1_{class9}$) and the *weighted average* (which uses the number of samples W_i in each class i, i.e., $F1_{class1} * W_1 + F1_{class2} * W_2 \cdots + F1_{class9} * W_9$).

It can be noted that on the validation fold continual updating does improve performance to some extent, especially under Recall and F1 score. Improvements in Recall are visible on the test fold as well. All in all the baseline appears able to extract information from the unlabelled data stream.

6.2   Results on Crowd Counting

Table 2 shows a quantitative analysis of the performance of the fine-tuned supervised model (*sup*) and two incrementally updated models (*upd*) on the validation and the test split, respectively, using the mean absolute error (MAE) metric.

The experiments were performed under three different experimental settings: (i) the initial model fine tuned on the supervised folds ($sup - ft$), (ii) a model incrementally updated on the validation fold ($upd - V$), and (iii) a model incrementally updated on both the validation and test folds considered as a single data stream ($upd - V + T$). In Table 2 all three models are tested on both the V and T portions of the data streams. The initial model was trained for 100 epochs on the supervised fold (S), whereas the incremental models were self-trained for 5 epochs in each session (we also tried 2 epochs with no significant change observed).

When compared with classical papers in the crowd counting literature, the MAE values in Table 2 are noticeable higher. Concretely, a recent work that incorporates optical flow to improve crowd counting achieved MAEs of 1.76, 0.97, and 1.78 on the FDST, UCSD, and Mall dataset, respectively [12]. Also, the original MCNN implementation yielded MAEs of 3.77 and 1.07 on FDST and UCSD (performance was not reported on Mall) [10,26]. The higher MAEs reported in our work are expected, due to the significantly different and more challenging training protocol (i.e., batch training in standard crowd counting work vs. continual learning here). For example, standard papers in crowd counting following the typical evaluation protocol employ 800 training images for the Mall and UCSD datasets; whereas, in our problem setting only 400 images are used for supervised training.

Previous batch results should be seen as upper bounds to our incremental task, whereas ours should be considered as new baselines for a new problem setting. While model updating does not seem to be effective (on average) on the validation streams, the effect is quite significant on the test fold (right side of the Table), with important performance gains.

7   Conclusions

In this paper we formulated the continual semi-supervised learning problem and proposed suitable training and testing protocols for it. To encourage future work in the area we created the first two benchmark datasets, as the foundations of our IJCAI 2021 challenge. We proposed a simple strategy based on batch self-training a baseline model in sessions. The results show that, in both the activity recognition and the crowd counting challenge, the baseline appears in fact to be able to extract information from the unlabelled data stream. Nevertheless, the need for a more sophisticated approach leveraging the dynamics of the data stream is clear.

References

1. Aljundi, R., Lin, M., Goujaud, B., Bengio, Y.: Gradient based sample selection for online continual learning. CoRR abs/1903.08671 (2019)
2. Bitarafan, A., Baghshah, M.S., Gheisari, M.: Incremental evolving domain adaptation. IEEE Trans. Knowl. Data Eng. **28**(8), 2128–2141 (2016)
3. Boominathan, L., Kruthiventi, S.S., Babu, R.V.: CrowdNet: a deep convolutional network for dense crowd counting. In: Proceedings of the 24th ACM International Conference on Multimedia, pp. 640–644 (2016)
4. Chan, A.B., Liang, Z.S.J., Vasconcelos, N.: Privacy preserving crowd monitoring: counting people without people models or tracking. In: 2008 IEEE Conference on Computer Vision and Pattern Recognition, pp. 1–7 (2008)
5. Chen, C., et al.: Progressive feature alignment for unsupervised domain adaptation. In: Proceedings of the IEEE Conference on Computer Vision and Pattern Recognition, pp. 627–636 (2019)
6. Chen, C., et al.: Progressive feature alignment for unsupervised domain adaptation. In: 2019 IEEE/CVF Conference on Computer Vision and Pattern Recognition (CVPR), pp. 627–636 (2019)
7. Chen, K., Loy, C.C., Gong, S., Xiang, T.: Feature mining for localised crowd counting. In: BMVC, vol. 1, p. 3 (2012)
8. Chen, Y., Li, W., Sakaridis, C., Dai, D., Gool, L.V.: Domain adaptive faster R-CNN for object detection in the wild. In: 2018 IEEE/CVF Conference on Computer Vision and Pattern Recognition, pp. 3339–3348 (2018)
9. Corona, K., Osterdahl, K., Collins, R., Hoogs, A.: MEVA: a large-scale multiview, multimodal video dataset for activity detection. In: Proceedings of the IEEE/CVF Winter Conference on Applications of Computer Vision, pp. 1060–1068 (2021)
10. Fang, Y., Zhan, B., Cai, W., Gao, S., Hu, B.: Locality-constrained spatial transformer network for video crowd counting. In: 2019 IEEE International Conference on Multimedia and Expo (ICME), pp. 814–819 (2019)
11. Farquhar, S., Gal, Y.: Towards robust evaluations of continual learning. ArXiv abs/1805.09733 (2018)
12. Hossain, M.A., Cannons, K., Jang, D., Cuzzolin, F., Xu, Z.: Video-based crowd counting using a multi-scale optical flow pyramid network. In: Proceedings of the Asian Conference on Computer Vision (2020)
13. Jiang, X., et al.: Crowd counting and density estimation by trellis encoder-decoder networks. In: Proceedings of the IEEE Conference on Computer Vision and Pattern Recognition, pp. 6133–6142 (2019)
14. Lange, M.D., et al.: Continual learning: a comparative study on how to defy forgetting in classification tasks. CoRR abs/1909.08383 (2019). https://arxiv.org/abs/1909.08383
15. Liu, W., Salzmann, M., Fua, P.: Estimating people flows to better count them in crowded scenes. CoRR abs/1911.10782 (2019). https://arxiv.org/abs/1911.10782

16. Lomonaco, V., Maltoni, D.: CORe50: a new dataset and benchmark for continuous object recognition. In: Conference on Robot Learning, pp. 17–26. PMLR (2017)
17. Mallya, A., Lazebnik, S.: PackNet: adding multiple tasks to a single network by iterative pruning. In: 2018 IEEE/CVF Conference on Computer Vision and Pattern Recognition, pp. 7765–7773 (2018)
18. Prabhu, A., Torr, P.H.S., Dokania, P.K.: GDumb: a simple approach that questions our progress in continual learning. In: Vedaldi, A., Bischof, H., Brox, T., Frahm, J.-M. (eds.) ECCV 2020. LNCS, vol. 12347, pp. 524–540. Springer, Cham (2020). https://doi.org/10.1007/978-3-030-58536-5_31
19. Rosenberg, C., Hebert, M., Schneiderman, H.: Semi-supervised self-training of object detection models (2005)
20. Tan, M., Le, Q.: EfficientNet: rethinking model scaling for convolutional neural networks. In: International Conference on Machine Learning, pp. 6105–6114. PMLR (2019)
21. Triguero, I., García, S., Herrera, F.: Self-labeled techniques for semi-supervised learning: taxonomy, software and empirical study. Knowl. Inf. Syst. **42**(2), 245–284 (2013). https://doi.org/10.1007/s10115-013-0706-y
22. Tzeng, E., Hoffman, J., Saenko, K., Darrell, T.: Adversarial discriminative domain adaptation. In: 2017 IEEE Conference on Computer Vision and Pattern Recognition (CVPR), pp. 2962–2971 (2017)
23. Van de Ven, G.M., Tolias, A.S.: Three scenarios for continual learning. arXiv preprint arXiv:1904.07734 (2019)
24. Xiong, F., Shi, X., Yeung, D.Y.: Spatiotemporal modeling for crowd counting in videos. In: 2017 IEEE International Conference on Computer Vision (ICCV), pp. 5161–5169 (2017). https://doi.org/10.1109/ICCV.2017.551
25. Xiong, H., Lu, H., Liu, C., Liu, L., Cao, Z., Shen, C.: From open set to closed set: counting objects by spatial divide-and-conquer. In: Proceedings of the IEEE International Conference on Computer Vision, pp. 8362–8371 (2019)
26. Zhang, Y., Zhou, D., Chen, S., Gao, S., Ma, Y.: Single-image crowd counting via multi-column convolutional neural network. In: Proceedings of the IEEE Conference on Computer Vision and Pattern Recognition, pp. 589–597 (2016)

Unsupervised Continual Learning
via Pseudo Labels

Jiangpeng He and Fengqing Zhu[✉]

Purdue Univeristy, West Lafayette, IN 47906, USA
{he416,zhu0}@purdue.edu

Abstract. Continual learning aims to learn new tasks incrementally using less computation and memory resources instead of retraining the model from scratch whenever new task arrives. However, existing approaches are designed in supervised fashion assuming all data from new tasks have been manually annotated, which are not practical for many real-life applications. In this work, we propose to use pseudo label instead of the ground truth to make continual learning feasible in unsupervised mode. The pseudo labels of new data are obtained by applying global clustering algorithm and we propose to use the model updated from last incremental step as the feature extractor. Due to the scarcity of existing work, we introduce a new benchmark experimental protocol for unsupervised continual learning of image classification task under class-incremental setting where no class label is provided for each incremental learning step. Our method is evaluated on the CIFAR-100 and ImageNet (ILSVRC) datasets by incorporating the pseudo label with various existing supervised approaches and show promising results in unsupervised scenario.

Keywords: Continual learning · Unsupervised learning · Pseudo label

1 Introduction

The success of many deep learning techniques rely on the following two assumptions: 1) training data is identically and independently distributed (*i.i.d.*), which rarely happens if new data and tasks arrive sequentially over time, 2) labels for the training data are available, which requires additional data annotation by human effort, and can be noisy as well. Continual learning has been proposed to tackle issue #1, which aims at learning new tasks incrementally without forgetting the knowledge on all tasks seen so far. Unsupervised learning focuses on addressing issue #2 to learn visual representations used for downstream tasks directly from unlabeled data. However, unsupervised continual learning, which is expected to tackle both issues mentioned above, has not been well studied [16]. Therefore, we introduce a simple yet effective method in this work that can be adapted by existing supervised continual learning approaches in unsupervised setting where no class label is required during the learning phase. We focuses on image classification task under the class-incremental setting [7] and the objective is to learn from unlabeled data for each incremental step while providing semantic meaningful clusters on all classes seen so far during inference. Figure 1 illustrates the difference

F. Cuzzolin et al. (Eds.): CSSL 2021, LNAI 13418, pp. 15–32, 2022.
https://doi.org/10.1007/978-3-031-17587-9_2

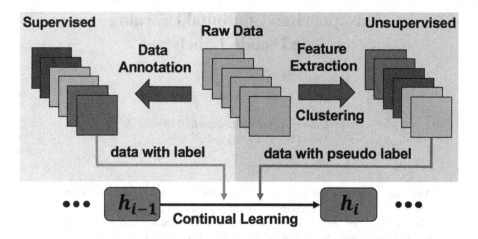

Fig. 1. Supervised vs. unsupervised continual learning for the new task i. h refers to the model in different incremental steps. The supervised and our proposed pseudo label based unsupervised continual learning are illustrated by green and red arrows respectively. (Color figure online)

between the typical supervised and proposed unsupervised continual learning scenarios to learn a new task i.

Current continual learning approaches can be generally summarized into three categories including (1) *Regularization based*, (2) *Bias-correction based* and (3) *Rehearsal based*. Our proposed method can be directly embedded into existing supervised approaches in category (1) and (2) with an additional step to extract features of unlabeled data and perform clustering to obtain pseudo label. However, for methods in (3), selecting exemplars from learned tasks when class label is not provided in unsupervised scenario is still an unsolved and challenging step. In this work, we tackle this issue by sampling the unlabeled data from the centroid of each generated cluster as exemplars to incorporate with *Rehearsal based* approaches.

Pseudo label [11] is widely applied in both semi-supervised and unsupervised learning scenarios to handle unlabeled data for downstream tasks, which is effective due to its simplicity, generality and ease of implementation. However, whether it is feasible for continual learning to rely on pseudo labels instead of human annotations is not well unexplored yet, which is more challenging as we also need to address catastrophic forgetting [17] in addition to learning new knowledge from unlabeled data.

In this work, we adopt K-means [13] as our global clustering algorithm for illustration purpose and we propose to use the continual learning model (except the last fully connected layers) at every incremental step for feature extraction of unlabeled data to obtain pseudo label. The exemplars used for *Rehearsal based* approaches are selected after applying k-means from each generated cluster based on the distance to cluster centroid without requiring the class labels. Note that we are not proposing new approach to address catastrophic forgetting for continual learning in this work, but instead we test the effectiveness of using pseudo labels to make existing supervised methods feasible in unsupervised setting. Therefore, we incorporate our method with existing representative supervised approaches from all three categories mentioned above including LWF [12], ICARL [20], EEIL [2], LUCIR [6], WA [28] and ILIO [3]. We show promising performance in unsupervised scenario on both CIFAR-100 [9] and ImageNet (ILSVRC) [22] datasets compared with results in supervised case that do require the ground truth for continual learning. The main contributions of this paper are summarized as follows.

- We explore a novel problem for continual learning using pseudo labels instead of human annotations, which is both challenging and meaningful for real-life applications.
- Our proposed method can be easily adapted by existing supervised continual learning techniques and we achieve competitive performance on both CIFAR-100 and ImageNet in unsupervised scenario.
- A new benchmark evaluation protocol is introduced for future research work and extensive experiments are conducted to analyze the effectiveness of each component in our proposed method.

2   Related Work

2.1   Continual Learning

The major challenge for continual learning is catastrophic forgetting [17] where the model quickly forgets already learned knowledge due to the unavailability of old data during the learning phase of new tasks. Many effective techniques have been proposed to address catastrophic forgetting in supervised scenario, which can be divided into three main categories: (1) *Regularization based* methods aim to retain old knowledge by constraining the change of parameters that are important for old tasks. Knowledge distillation loss [5] is one of the representatives, which was first applied in [12] to transfer knowledge using soft target distribution from teacher model to student model. Later the variants of distillation loss proposed in [3,6] are shown to be more effective by using stronger constraints. (2) *Bias-correction based* strategy aims to maintain the model performance by correcting the biased parameters towards new tasks in the classifier. Wu *et al.* [26] proposed to apply an additional linear layer with a validation sets after each incremental step. Weight Aligning (WA) is proposed in [28] to directly correct the biased weights in the FC layer, which does not require extra parameters compared with previous one. (3) *Rehearsal based* methods [2,20] use partial data from old tasks to periodically remind model of already learned knowledge to mitigate forgetting.

However, all these methods require class label for the continual learning process, which limits their applications in real world. Therefore, in this work we propose to use pseudo label obtained from cluster assignments to make existing supervised approaches feasible in unsupervised mode.

2.2   Unsupervised Representation Learning

Many approaches have been proposed to learn visual representation using deep models with no supervision. *Clustering* is one type of unsupervised learning methods that has been extensively studied in computer vision problems [1,27], which requires little domain knowledge from unlabeled data compared with self-supervised learning [8]. Caron *et al.* [1] proposed to iteratively cluster features and update model with subsequently assigned pseudo labels obtained by applying standard clustering algorithm such as K-means [13]. The most recent work [27] propose to perform clustering and model update simultaneously to address the model's instability during training phase. However, all these existing methods only work on static datasets and are not capable of learning new knowledge incrementally. In addition, the idea of using pseudo label is also rarely explored under continual learning context where the learning environment changes a lot since we need to address catastrophic forgetting as well besides learning visual representation from unlabeled data. In this work, we propose to use the fixed pseudo label for unsupervised continual learning which is described in Sect. 4. We also show in Sect. 5.5 that iteratively perform clustering to update pseudo labels will result in performance degradation under continual learning context.

3   Problem Setup

Continual learning aims to learn knowledge from a sequence of new tasks. Broadly speaking, it can be divided into (1) task-incremental, (2) domain-incremental, and (3) class-incremental as discussed in [7]. Methods designed for task-incremental problems use a multi-head classifier for each independent task and domain-incremental methods aim to learn the label shift instead of new classes. In this work, we study the unsupervised scenario under class-incremental setting, which is also known as Single-Incremental-Task [15] using a single-head classifier for inference. Specifically, the class-incremental learning problem $\mathcal{T}$ can be formulated as learning a sequence of N tasks $\{\mathcal{T}^1, ..., \mathcal{T}^N\}$ corresponding to $N-1$ incremental steps since the learning of the first task $\mathcal{T}^1$ is not related to incremental regime as no previous knowledge need to maintain. Each task $\mathcal{T}^i \in \mathcal{T}$ for $i \in \{1, ...N\}$ contains M^i non-overlapped new classes to learn. In this work, we study class-incremental learning in unsupervised scenario starting from task $\mathcal{T}^2$ for incremental steps only where we assume the initial model is supervisedly trained on $\mathcal{T}^1$. Let $\{D^1, ..., D^N\}$ denotes the training data corresponds to N tasks, where D^i indicates the data belonging to the task i. In supervised case, $D^i = \{(\mathbf{x}_1^i, y_1^i)...(\mathbf{x}_{n_i}^i, y_{n_i}^i)\}$ where $\mathbf{x}$ and y represent the data and the label respectively, and n_i refers to the number of total training data in D^i. In unsupervised case, we assume the labels of data are unknown for each incremental step so $D^i = \{\mathbf{x}_1^i...\mathbf{x}_{n_i}^i\}$ for $i \in \{2, 3, ...N\}$. The objective is to learn from unlabeled data for each incremental step while providing semantic meaningful clusters after each step on test data belonging to all classes seen so far.

Fixed Step Size: As shown above M^i refers to the number of added new classes for task $\mathcal{T}^i \in \mathcal{T}$, which is also defined as incremental step size. Existing benchmark protocols [3,6,20] for supervised continual learning use a fixed step size M over all tasks where $M^i = M$ for $i \in 1, ...N$ and the continual learning under variable step size is not well studied yet even in supervised case. Therefore, we also assume that the number of new added classes for each task remain unchanged over the entire continual learning

---

Algorithm 1. Unsupervised Continual Learning

Input: a sequence of N tasks $\{\mathcal{T}^1, ..., \mathcal{T}^N\}$
Input: An initial model $\mathbf{h}_0$
Require: Clustering algorithm Θ
Output: Updated model $\mathbf{h}_N$
1:   $M^1 \leftarrow |\mathcal{T}^1|_{class}$ {Added classes in first task}
2:   $\mathbf{h}_1 \leftarrow Learning(\mathcal{T}^1, \mathbf{h}_0)$ {Learning first task}
3: **for** i = 2, ..., N **do**
4:     $M^i \leftarrow |\mathcal{T}^i|_{class}$ {number of new added classes}
5:     $D^i \leftarrow \{\mathbf{x}_1, ..., \mathbf{x}_{n_i}\}$ {Unlabeled training data in $\mathcal{T}^i$}
6:     $\mathbf{h}_{fe} \leftarrow \mathbf{h}_{i-1}$ {Feature extractor}
7:     $\{\tilde{a}_1,.. \tilde{a}_{n_i}\} \leftarrow \Theta(\mathbf{h}_{fe}(D^i))$ {Cluster assignments}
8:     $\tilde{Y}^i \leftarrow \{ \underset{k=1,...n_i}{\tilde{y}_k} = \tilde{a}_k + \sum\limits_{j=1}^{i-1} M^j \}$ {Pseudo label}
9:     $\mathbf{h}_i \leftarrow Continual\ Learning(D^i, \tilde{Y}^i, \mathbf{h}_{i-1})$
10: **end for**
11: **return** h^N

---

process, *i.e.* the fixed step size M is known in advance in our unsupervised setting while class labels of data in each incremental step are not provided.

Online and Offline Implementation: Based on training restriction, continual learning methods can be implemented as either online or offline where the former methods [3,14,19] use each data only once to update the model and the data can be used for multiple times in the offline case. In general, the online scenario is more closer to real life setting but is also more challenging to realize. In this work, our proposed method is implemented in both online and offline scenarios for unsupervised continual learning. Note that for our implementation in online case, we assume that we have access to all training data $\{\mathbf{x}_1^i...\mathbf{x}_{n_i}^i\} \in D^i$ before the learning of each new task i but we use each data only once to update the model.

4 Our Method

In this work, we propose a simple yet effective method for unsupervised continual learning using pseudo label obtained based on cluster assignments. The overall procedure to learn a sequence of new tasks $\{\mathcal{T}^1, ..., \mathcal{T}^N\}$ are illustrated in Algorithm 1. The updated model after learning each task is evaluated to provide semantic meaningful clusters on all classes seen so far.

For illustration purpose, we adopt k-means as our global clustering algorithm to generate cluster assignments and obtain pseudo label, which will be illustrated in Sect. 4.1. Then, we demonstrate how to easily incorporate our method with existing supervised approaches in Sect. 4.2.

4.1   Clustering: Obtain Pseudo Label

Clustering is one of the most common methods for unsupervised learning, which requires little domain knowledge compared with self-supervised techniques. We focus on using a general clustering method such as K-means [13], while we also provide the experimental results using other clustering methods as illustrated in *Appendix*, which indicates that the choice is not critical for continual learning performance in our setting. Specifically, K-means algorithm learns a centroid matrix C together with cluster assignments $\tilde{a}_k$ for each input data $\mathbf{x}_k$ by iteratively minimizing $\frac{1}{N}\sum_{k=1}^{N}||\mathbf{h}_{fe}(\mathbf{x}_k) - C\tilde{a}_k||_2^2$, where $\mathbf{h}_{fe}$ refers to the feature extractor. Let m and n represent the number of learned classes and new added classes respectively, then we have $\tilde{a}_k \in \{1, 2, ..., n\}$ and the pseudo label $\tilde{Y}$ for continual learning is obtained by $\{\tilde{y}_k = \tilde{a}_k + m | k = 1, 2, ..\}$ and $\tilde{y}_k \in \{m+1, m+2, ..., m+n\}$.

Learning visual representation from unlabeled data using pseudo label is proposed in [1], which iteratively performs clustering and updating the feature extractor. However, they are not capable of learning new classes incrementally and the learning environment changes under continual learning context as we need to maintain the learned knowledge as well as learning from new tasks. Therefore, in this work we propose to apply the model, $\mathbf{h}_{fe} = \mathbf{h}_{i-1}$, obtained after incremental step $i - 1$ (except the last fully connected layer) as the feature extractor for incremental step i to extract feature embeddings on all unlabeled data belonging to the new task. Next, we apply k-means based on extracted features to generate cluster assignments and use the fixed pseudo label $\tilde{Y}$ to learn from new task during the entire incremental learning step i. We show in our experiments later that alternatively performing clustering and use pseudo label to update the model as in [1] will result in performance degradation which is discussed in Sect. 5.5. Note that we assume $\mathbf{h}_1$ is obtained from $\mathcal{T}^1$ in supervised mode as illustrated in Sect. 3, so in this work we mainly focus on how to incrementally learn new classes from unlabeled data while maintaining performance on all old classes seen so far.

4.2   Incorporating into Supervised Approaches

The obtained pseudo label $\tilde{Y}$ can be easily incorporated with *Regularization-based* methods using knowledge distillation loss or its variants. The distillation loss is formulated by Eq. 1

$$L_D = \frac{1}{N}\sum_{k=1}^{N}\sum_{r=1}^{m} -\hat{p}_T^{(r)}(\mathbf{x}_k)log[p_T^{(r)}(\mathbf{x}_k)] \tag{1}$$

$$\hat{p}_T^{(r)} = \frac{\exp{(\hat{o}^{(r)}/T)}}{\sum_{j=1}^{m}\exp{(\hat{o}^{(j)}/T)}}, \quad p_T^{(r)} = \frac{\exp{(o^{(r)}/T)}}{\sum_{j=1}^{m}\exp{(o^{(j)}/T)}}$$

where $\hat{o}^{m\times 1}$ and $o^{m\times 1}$ denote the output logits of student and teacher models respectively for the m learned classes. T is the temperature scalar used to soften the probability distribution. The cross entropy loss to learn the added n new classes can be expressed as

$$L_C = \frac{1}{N} \sum_{k=1}^{N} \sum_{r=1}^{n+m} -\tilde{y}_k^{(r)} log[p^{(r)}(\mathbf{x}_k)] \tag{2}$$

where $\tilde{y}_k \in \tilde{Y}$ is the obtained pseudo label for data $\mathbf{x}_k$ instead of the ground truth labels in supervised case. Then the cross-distillation loss combining cross entropy L_C and distillation L_D is formulated in Eq. 3 with a hyper-parameter $\alpha = \frac{m}{m+n}$ to tune the influence between two terms.

$$L_{CD}(\mathbf{x}) = \alpha L_D(\mathbf{x}) + (1 - \alpha)L_C(\mathbf{x}) \tag{3}$$

Herding dynamic algorithm [24] is widely applied for *Rehearsal based* methods to select exemplars based on class mean in supervised case. However, since no class label is provided in unsupervised scenario, we instead propose to select exemplars based on cluster mean. Algorithm 2 describes exemplar selection step for task $\mathcal{T}^i$. The exemplar set Q stores the data and pseudo label pair denoted as $(\mathbf{x}_k, \tilde{y}_k)$.

The incorporation with *Bias-correction based* methods is the most straightforward. BIC [26] applies an additional linear model for bias correction after each incremental step using a small validation set containing balanced old and new class data. In our unsupervised scenario, both the training and validation set used to estimate bias can be constructed using obtained pseudo label instead of the ground truth. The most recent work WA [28] calculates the norms of weights vectors in FC layer for old and new class respectively and use the ratio to correct bias without requiring extra parameters. Thus our method can be directly embedded with it by an addition step to obtain pseudo label as illustrated in Sect. 4.1.

We emphasize that we are not introducing new method to address catastrophic forgetting, but rather investigating whether it is possible to use pseudo labels instead of ground truth labels for continual learning. We show in Sect. 5 that our proposed method works effectively with existing approaches from all categories mentioned above.

5   Experimental Results

In this section, we evaluate our proposed method from two perspectives. 1) We incorporate with existing approaches and compare results obtained in unsupervised and supervised cases to show the ability of using pseudo labels for unsupervised continual learning to provide semantic meaningful clusters for all classes seen so far. 2) We analyze the effectiveness of each component in our proposed method including the exemplar selection and the choice of feature extractor in unsupervised scenario. These experimental results are presented and discussed in Sects. 5.4 and 5.5, respectively. (Additional results are available in *Appendix*).

5.1   Benchmark Experimental Protocol

Although different benchmark experimental protocols are proposed in supervised scenario [3,6,20], there is no agreed protocol for evaluation of unsupervised continual learning methods. In addition, various learning environments may happen when class

---

Algorithm 2. Unsupervised Exemplar Selection

Input: image set $D^i = \{\mathbf{x}_1, ..., \mathbf{x}_{ni}\}$ from task $\mathcal{T}^i$
Input: q target exemplars per class
Require: clustering algorithm Θ
Require: feature extractor $\mathbf{h}_{fe} = \mathbf{h}_i$
Output: Exemplar set Q
1: $M^i \leftarrow |\mathcal{T}^i|_{class}$ {number of new added classes}
2: $\{\tilde{a}_1,.. \tilde{a}_{n_i}\} \leftarrow \Theta(\mathbf{h}_{fe}(D^i))$ {Cluster assignments}
3: **for** j = 1, 2,..., M_i **do**
4:      $\mathbf{X}_j \leftarrow \{\mathbf{x}_n | \tilde{a}_n = j\}$
5:      $\mu_j \leftarrow \frac{1}{|\mathbf{X}_j|} \sum_{\mathbf{x} \in \mathbf{X}_j} \mathbf{h}_{fe}(\mathbf{x})$ {Cluster mean}
6:      **for** k = 1, 2,..., q **do**
7:          $\mathbf{e}_k \leftarrow \underset{\mathbf{x} \in \mathbf{X}_j}{argmin}\{\mu_j - \frac{1}{k}[\mathbf{h}_{fe}(\mathbf{x}) + \sum_{l=1}^{k-1} \mathbf{h}_{fe}(\mathbf{e}_l)]\}$ {herding selection [24] within cluster}
8:      **end for**
9:      $Q \leftarrow Q \cup \{\mathbf{e}_1, ..., \mathbf{e}_q\}$
10: **end for**
11: **return** Q

---

label is not available so it is impossible to use one protocol to evaluate upon all potential scenarios. Thus, our proposed new protocol focuses on class-incremental learning setting and aims to evaluate the ability of unsupervised methods to learn from unlabeled data while maintaining the learned knowledge during continual learning. Specifically, the following assumptions are made: (1) all the new data belong to new class, (2) the number of new added class (step size) is fixed and known beforehand, (3) no class label is provided for learning (except for the initial step) and (4) the updated model should be able to provide semantic meaningful clusters for all classes seen so far during inference. Our protocol is introduced based on current research progress for supervised class-incremental learning and three benchmark datasets are considered including (i) CIFAR-100 [9] with step size 5, 10, 20, 50 (ii) ImageNet-1000 (ILSVRC) [22] with step size 100 and (iii) ImageNet-100 (100 classes subset of ImageNet-1000) with step size 10. Top-1 and Top-5 ACC are used for CIFAR-100 and ImageNet, respectively.

5.2 Evaluation Metrics

We evaluate our method using cluster accuracy (ACC), which is widely applied in unsupervised setting [1,23] when class label is not provided. We first find the most represented class label for each cluster using Hungarian matching algorithm [10], and then calculate the accuracy as $\frac{N_c}{N}$ where N is the total number of data and N_c is the number of correctly classified data. Note that the classification accuracy used in supervised setting is consistent with cluster accuracy and is widely used for performance comparison in unsupervised case as in [23]. In this work, ACC is used to evaluate the model's ability to provide semantic meaningful clusters.

Table 1. Summary of unsupervised results and the comparison with supervised case. The average ACC (Avg) over all incremental steps and the last step ACC (Last) are reported. w/ and w/o denote with or without label for continual learning, *i.e.* supervised or unsupervised. $\{\Delta = w/ - w/o\}$ shows the performance difference. Spotlight results ($|\Delta| < 0.05$) for Avg accuracy are marked in bold.

Datasets	CIFAR-100								ImageNet			
Step size	5		10		20		50		10		100	
ACC	Avg	Last	Avg	Last	Avg	Last	Avg	Last	Avg	Last	Avg	Last
LWF (w/)	0.299	0.155	0.393	0.240	0.465	0.352	0.512	0.512	0.602	0.391	0.528	0.374
LWF+Ours (w/o, Δ)	−0.071	−0.029	−0.091	−0.025	−0.086	−0.062	−0.095	−0.095	**−0.033**	−0.053	−0.211	−0.174
ICARL (w/)	0.606	0.461	0.626	0.518	0.641	0.565	0.607	0.607	0.821	0.644	0.608	0.440
ICARL+Ours (w/o, Δ)	−0.084	−0.045	−0.135	−0.142	−0.158	−0.174	−0.108	−0.108	**−0.043**	−0.047	−0.197	−0.015
EEIL (w/)	0.643	0.482	0.638	0.517	0.637	0.565	0.603	0.603	0.893	0.805	0.696	0.520
EEIL+Ours (w/o, Δ)	−0.071	−0.043	−0.131	−0.121	−0.131	−0.148	−0.088	−0.088	**−0.040**	−0.064	−0.199	−0.154
LUCIR (w/)	0.623	0.478	0.631	0.521	0.647	0.589	0.642	0.642	0.898	0.835	0.834	0.751
LUCIR+Ours (w/o, Δ)	**−0.015**	−0.003	−0.104	−0.106	−0.131	−0.152	−0.111	−0.111	**−0.037**	−0.083	−0.293	−0.342
WA (w/)	0.643	0.496	0.649	0.535	0.669	0.592	0.655	0.655	0.905	0.841	0.859	0.811
WA+Ours (w/o, Δ)	**−0.034**	−0.014	−0.110	−0.106	−0.121	−0.136	−0.092	−0.092	**−0.037**	−0.056	−0.295	−0.376
ILIO (w/)	0.664	0.515	0.676	0.564	0.681	0.621	0.652	0.652	0.903	0.845	0.696	0.601
ILIO+Ours (w/o, Δ)	−0.123	−0.194	−0.140	−0.175	−0.134	−0.157	−0.106	−0.106	−0.057	−0.118	−0.178	−0.212

5.3   Implementation Detail

Our implementation is based on Pytorch [18] and we use ResNet-32 for CIFAR-100 and ResNet-18 for ImageNet. The ResNet implementation follows the setting as suggested in [4]. The setting of incorporated existing approaches follows their own repositories. We select $q = 20$ exemplars per cluster to construct exemplar set and arrange classes using identical random seed (1993) with benchmark supervised experiment protocol [20]. We ran five times for each experiment and the average performance is reported.

5.4   Incorporating with Supervised Approaches

In this part, our method is evaluated by incorporated into existing supervised methods including **LWF** [12], **ICARL** [20], **EEIL** [2], **LUCIR** [6], **WA** [28] and **ILIO** [3], which are representative methods from all *Regularization based, Bias-correction based* and *Rehearsal based* categories as described in Sect. 2. Note that **ILIO** is implemented in online scenario where each data is used only once to update model while others are implemented in offline. We embed the pseudo label as illustrated in Sect. 4 to evaluate the performance of selected approaches in unsupervised mode. *E.g.* **ICARL + Ours** denotes the implementation of **ICARL** in unsupervised mode by incorporating with our proposed method. Table 1 summarizes results in terms of last step ACC (Last) and average ACC (Avg) calculated by averaging ACC for all incremental steps, which shows overall performance for the entire continual learning procedure. We also report the performance difference $\Delta = w/ - w/o$ and observe only small degradation by comparing unsupervised results with supervised results. In addition, we calculate the average accuracy drop by $Avg(\Delta) = Avg(w/) - Avg(w/o)$ for each incremental step corresponds to each method. The $Avg(\Delta)$ ranges from $[0.015, 0.295]$ with an average of 0.114. Our

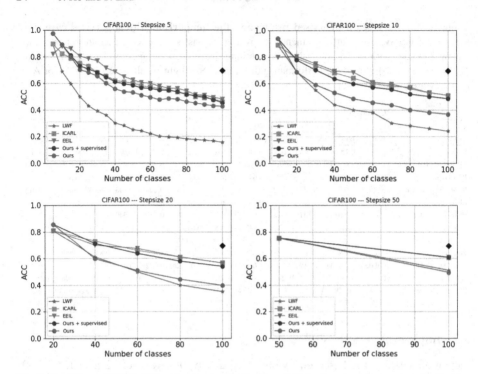

Fig. 2. Results on CIFAR-100 with step size 5, 10, 20, and 50 by incorporating our method with existing approaches to realize continual learning in unsupervised scenario. (Best viewed in color) (Color figure online)

method can work well with but not limited to these selected representative methods and we achieve competitive performance in unsupervised scenario without requiring human annotated labels during continual learning phase. Figure 2 shows cluster accuracy for each incremental step on CIFAR-100. (More results and discussion are available in the *Appendix*).

5.5 Ablation Study

We conduct extensive experiments to **1)** analyze the unsupervised exemplar selection step as described in Sect. 4.2 by varying the number of exemplars per class and compare the results with random selection. **2)** Study the impacts of different methods that can be used to extract feature for clustering to obtain pseudo label during continual learning. For both experiments, we first construct our baseline method denoted as **Ours**, which uses distillation loss as described in Eq. 3 and exemplars from learned tasks as described in Algorithm 2. (see implementation detail in *Appendix*).

Table 2. Ablation study for different approaches to obtain pseudo labels on CIFAR-100 and ImageNet in terms of average ACC (Avg) and last step ACC (Last). The best results are marked in bold.

Datasets	CIFAR-100								ImageNet			
Step size	5		10		20		50		10		100	
ACC	Avg	Last	Avg	Last	Avg	Last	Avg	Last	Avg	Last	Avg	Last
Scratch	0.106	0.038	0.095	0.015	0.122	0.038	0.226	0.226	0.282	0.158	0.069	0.023
PCA	0.156	0.085	0.143	0.061	0.171	0.083	0.287	0.287	0.308	0.175	/	/
FFE	0.459	0.338	0.399	0.281	0.401	0.323	0.392	0.392	0.757	0.620	0.405	0.275
UPL-10	0.498	0.376	0.415	0.293	0.430	0.320	0.401	0.401	0.797	0.653	0.446	0.294
UPL-20	0.523	0.394	0.422	0.296	0.445	0.339	0.413	0.413	0.816	0.699	0.458	0.311
UPL-30	0.513	0.383	0.435	0.324	0.459	0.364	0.433	0.433	0.832	0.705	0.460	0.332
Ours	**0.558**	**0.426**	**0.482**	**0.368**	**0.486**	**0.397**	**0.495**	**0.495**	**0.849**	**0.722**	**0.471**	**0.342**

For part 1), we vary the target number of exemplars per class $q \in \{10, 20, 50, 100\}$ and compare the results with random exemplar selection from each generated cluster, denoted as **Random**. The results on CIFAR-100 are shown in Fig. 3. We observe that the overall performance will be improved by increasing q even using randomly selected exemplars. In addition, our proposed method, which selects exemplars based on cluster mean, outperforms **Random** by a larger margin when q becomes larger.

For part 2), we compare our method using the updated model from last incremental step as feature extractor as illustrated in Algorithm 1 with i) **Scratch**: apply a scratch model with the same network architecture as feature extractor, ii) **PCA**: directly apply PCA algorithm [25] on input images to obtain feature embeddings for clustering, iii) **Fixed Feature Extractor (FFE)**: use model h_1 as described in Sect. 4.1 as the fixed feature extractor for the entire continual learning process, iv) **Updated Pseudo Label (UPL-K)**: iteratively update model and perform clustering within each incremental step as proposed in [1], where K indicates how frequently we update the pseudo label e.g. UPL - 10 means we update pseudo label for every 10 epochs. All these variants are modified based on our baseline method. Results are summarized in Table 2. The scratch method provides lower bound performance and FFE outperforms PCA by a large margin, showing the advanced ability of using deep models to extract more discriminative feature for clustering. Note that we did not perform PCA on ImageNet-1000 as it takes quite a long time for computation. Comparing UPL-K with $K = 0, 10, 20, 30$ ($K = 0$ is Ours), we observe that if the updating frequency increases (K decreases), the overall performance degrades. As discussed in Sect. 4.1, different from unsupervised representation learning that uses a model from scratch, in continual learning we also need to preserve the learned knowledge for all classes seen so far and update pseudo label repeatedly will accelerate the catastrophic forgetting, resulting in the performance drop.

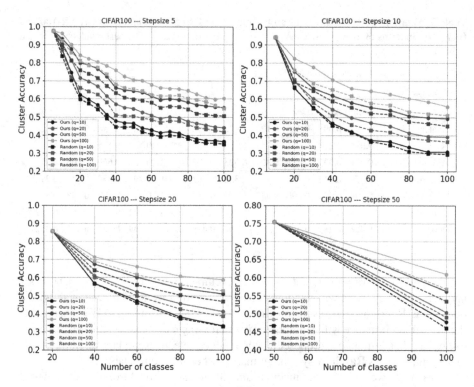

Fig. 3. Results on CIFAR-100 by varying target exemplar size $q \in \{10, 20, 50, 100\}$ and comparison with random selection.

6 Conclusion

In summary, we explore a novel problem of unsupervised continual learning under class-incremental setting where the objective is to learn new classes incrementally while providing semantic meaningful clusters on all classes seen so far. We proposed a simple yet effective method using pseudo labels obtained based on cluster assignments to learn from unlabeled data for each incremental step. We introduced a new experimental protocol and evaluate our method on benchmark image classification datasets including CIFAR-100 and ImageNet (ILSVRC). We demonstrate that our method can be easily embedded with various existing supervised approaches implemented under both online and offline modes to achieve competitive performance in unsupervised scenario. Finally, we show that our proposed exemplar selection method works effectively without requiring ground truth and iteratively updating pseudo labels will cause performance degradation under continual learning context.

Appendix

Implementation Detail For Our Baseline Method

In the paper, we conduct extensive experiments in Sect. 5.5 using a baseline solution denoted as **Ours**. The overview of our baseline method is shown in Fig. 4, which

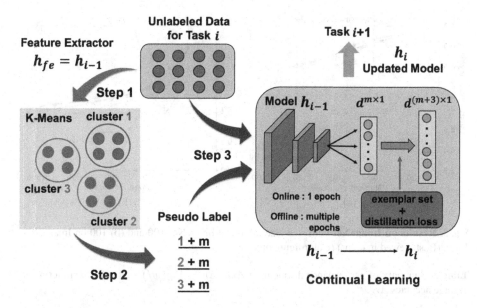

Fig. 4. Overview of our baseline solution to learn the new task i. h refers to the model in different steps and **m** denotes the number of learned classes so far after task $i - 1$. Firstly, we apply $\mathbf{h}_{i-1}$ (except the last fully connected layer) to extract feature embeddings used for K-means clustering where the number **1, 2, 3** denote the corresponding cluster assignments. In step 2 we obtain the pseudo label **1 + m, 2 + m, 3 + m** respectively. Finally in step 3, the unlabeled data with pseudo label is used together for continual learning.

incorporates pseudo labels introduced in Sect. 4.1 with knowledge distillation loss as in Eq. 3 and exemplar replay as described in Algorithm 2. Thus, the difference between our baseline solution and **EEIL** [2] is that we exclude data augmentation and balanced fine-tuning steps.

We apply ResNet-32 for CIFAR and ResNet-18 for ImageNet, which keeps same with in Sect. 5.3. We use batch size of 128 with initial learning rate of 0.1. SGD optimizer is applied with weight decay of 0.00001. We train 120 epochs for each incremental step and the learning rate is decreased by $1/10$ for every 30 epochs. We perform each experiment 5 times and the average results are reported in Table 2 and Fig. 3.

Additional Experimental Results

In this section, we show additional experiment results for (1) cluster accuracy for each incremental step on ImageNet [22]. (2) Analysis of performance drop compared with supervised results corresponds to Table 1. (3) Impact of different clustering algorithms by comparing K-means clustering [13] with Gaussian Mixture Models (GMM) [21]. (4) Results in terms of other evaluation metrics including *Normalized Mutual Information* (NMI) and *Adjusted Rand Index* (ARI). Both experiments are implemented by using our **baseline** solution on test data of CIFAR-100 with step size 5, 10, 20, 50.

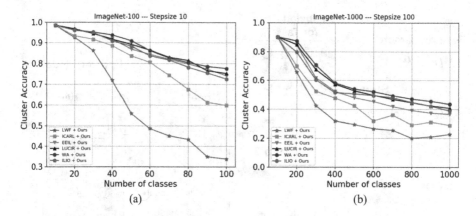

Fig. 5. Results on ImageNet with step size (a) 10 on ImageNet-100 and (b) 100 on ImageNet-1000. (Best viewed in color) (Color figure online)

Table 3. Summary of performance degradation $Avg(\Delta) = Avg(w/) - Avg(w/o)$ in terms of average accuracy Avg.

Datasets	CIFAR-100				ImageNet	
Step size	5	10	20	50	10	100
LWF	−0.071	−0.091	−0.086	−0.095	−0.033	−0.211
ICARL	−0.084	−0.132	−0.158	−0.108	−0.043	−0.197
EEIL	−0.071	−0.131	−0.131	−0.088	−0.040	−0.199
LUCIR	−0.015	−0.104	−0.131	−0.111	−0.037	−0.293
WA	−0.034	−0.110	−0.121	−0.092	−0.037	−0.295
ILIO	−0.123	−0.140	−0.134	−0.106	−0.057	−0.178

Results on ImageNet. The cluster accuracy evaluated after each incremental step on CIFAR-100 [9] with different step sizes are shown in Fig. 2 and in this part we provide the results on ImageNet with step size 10 and 100 as shown in Fig. 5.

Analysis of Performance Drop. In Sect. 5.4, we incorporate our method with existing supervised approaches and results are shown in Table 1. In this part, we further investigate the performance degradation in unsupervised scenario. Specifically, we calculate the average accuracy drop by $Avg(\Delta) = Avg(w/) - Avg(w/o)$ for each incremental step corresponds to each method. The results are shown in Table 3 where $Avg(\Delta)$ ranges from $[0.015, 0.295]$ with an average of 0.114. We notice that the performance degradation for each incremental step do not vary a lot for different approaches. Therefore, the methods with higher accuracy in supervised case are more likely to achieve higher performance in unsupervised scenario by incorporating with our pseudo labels. In addition, the performance degradation will increase in online scenario (ILIO) as well as for very large incremental step size (100), which are both challenging cases even in supervised continual learning with human annotations.

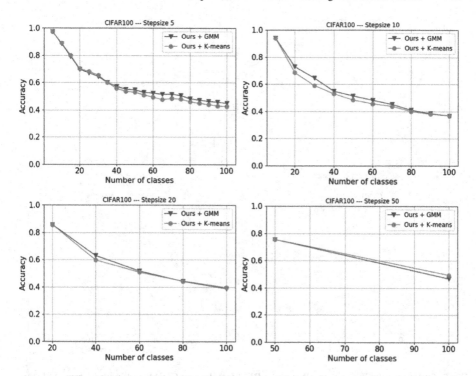

Fig. 6. Results of test data on CIFAR-100 for comparing K-means and GMM with incremental step size (a) 5, 10, 20 and 50. The Accuracy refers to cluster accuracy (ACC). (Best viewed in color) (Color figure online)

K-Means vs. GMM. As illustrated in Sect. 4, our proposed method use K-means clustering for illustration purpose to obtain the pseudo labels and to sample exemplars. In this part, we show the results in terms of cluster accuracy (ACC) for each incremental step by comparing K-means with GMMs, which estimates the parameters of each Gaussian distribution through expectation-maximization algorithm. Figure 6 shows the ACC results on CIFAR-100 with step size 5, 10, 20 and 50. We observe only small performance difference for all incremental steps, which shows that the choice of clustering methods are not crucial for our proposed method.

Results Evaluated By NMI and ARI. In the paper we use cluster accuracy (ACC) to evaluate the model's ability to provide semantic meaningful cluster on test data as illustrated Sect. 5.2. In this part, in addition to ACC, we also provide results in terms of NMI and ARI to measure the quality of obtained semantic meaningful clusters. Let A and B refer to ground truth labels and generated cluster assignments.

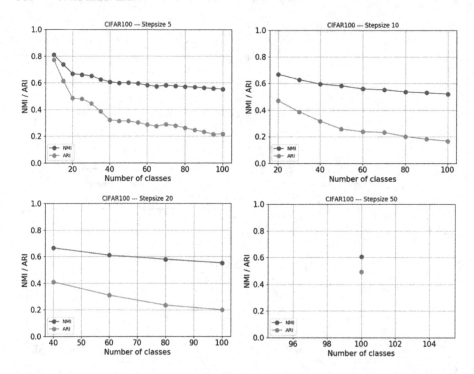

Fig. 7. Offline results in terms of NMI and ARI of test data on CIFAR-100 with incremental step size 5, 10, 20 and 50. The Accuracy refers to cluster accuracy (ACC). Note that only unsupervised incremental results (starting from task 2) are reported in this part. (Best viewed in color) (Color figure online)

NMI measures the shared information between two clustering assignments A and B by

$$NMI(A, B) = \frac{I(A, B)}{\sqrt{H(A)H(B)}}$$

where $H(\cdot)$ and $I(\cdot)$ denote entropy and mutual information, respectively.

ARI is defined by

$$ARI(A, B) = \frac{\sum_{i,j} \binom{N_{i,j}}{2} - \frac{\sum_i \binom{N_i}{2} \sum_j \binom{N_j}{2}}{\binom{N}{2}}}{\frac{1}{2}[\sum_i \binom{N_i}{2} + \sum_j \binom{N_j}{2}] - \frac{\sum_i \binom{N_i}{2} \sum_j \binom{N_j}{2}}{\binom{N}{2}}}$$

where $\binom{N}{2}$ refers to binomial coefficients and N is the total number of data in the cluster. N_i and N_j denote number of data with cluster assignment C_i in B and the number of data with class label C_j^* in A, respectively. Ni, j is the number of data with the class label $C_j^* \in A$ assigned to cluster assignment $C_i \in B$.

NMI and ARI ranges from $[0, 1]$ and 1 means a perfect match. Figure 7 shows the results on CIFAR-100 with incremental step size 5, 10, 20, and 50 using our baseline method. We observe consistent performance compared with using cluster accuracy (ACC) as metric as shown in Fig. 2 in paper. Note that both results are reported starting from the second task (first incremental step).

References

1. Caron, M., Bojanowski, P., Joulin, A., Douze, M.: Deep clustering for unsupervised learning of visual features. In: Proceedings of the European Conference on Computer Vision (2018)
2. Castro, F.M., Marin-Jimenez, M.J., Guil, N., Schmid, C., Alahari, K.: End-to-end incremental learning. In: Proceedings of the European Conference on Computer Vision (2018)
3. He, J., Mao, R., Shao, Z., Zhu, F.: Incremental learning in online scenario. In: Proceedings of the IEEE Conference on Computer Vision and Pattern Recognition, pp. 13926–13935 (2020)
4. He, K., Zhang, X., Ren, S., Sun, J.: Deep residual learning for image recognition. In: Proceedings of the IEEE Conference on Computer Vision and Pattern Recognition, pp. 770–778 (2016)
5. Hinton, G., Vinyals, O., Dean, J.: Distilling the knowledge in a neural network. In: Proceedings of the NIPS Deep Learning and Representation Learning Workshop (2015). https://arxiv.org/abs/1503.02531
6. Hou, S., Pan, X., Loy, C.C., Wang, Z., Lin, D.: Learning a unified classifier incrementally via rebalancing. In: Proceedings of the IEEE Conference on Computer Vision and Pattern Recognition, pp. 831–839 (2019)
7. Hsu, Y.C., Liu, Y.C., Ramasamy, A., Kira, Z.: Re-evaluating continual learning scenarios: a categorization and case for strong baselines. arXiv preprint arXiv:1810.12488 (2018)
8. Jing, L., Tian, Y.: Self-supervised visual feature learning with deep neural networks: a survey. IEEE Trans. Pattern Anal. Mach. Intell. **43**(11), 4037–4058 (2020)
9. Krizhevsky, A., Hinton, G., et al.: Learning multiple layers of features from tiny images (2009)
10. Kuhn, H.W.: The Hungarian method for the assignment problem. Naval Res. Logist. Q. **2**(1–2), 83–97 (1955)
11. Lee, D.H., et al.: Pseudo-label: the simple and efficient semi-supervised learning method for deep neural networks. In: Workshop on Challenges in Representation Learning, ICML (2013)
12. Li, Z., Hoiem, D.: Learning without forgetting. IEEE Trans. Pattern Anal. Mach. Intell. **40**(12), 2935–2947 (2017)
13. Lloyd, S.: Least squares quantization in PCM. IEEE Trans. Inf. Theory **28**(2), 129–137 (1982)
14. Lopez-Paz, D., Ranzato, M.: Gradient episodic memory for continual learning. In: Advances in Neural Information Processing Systems, pp. 6467–6476 (2017)
15. Maltoni, D., Lomonaco, V.: Continuous learning in single-incremental-task scenarios. Neural Netw. **116**, 56–73 (2019)

16. Masana, M., Liu, X., Twardowski, B., Menta, M., Bagdanov, A.D., van de Weijer, J.: Class-incremental learning: survey and performance evaluation. arXiv preprint arXiv:2010.15277 (2020)

17. McCloskey, M., Cohen, N.J.: Catastrophic interference in connectionist networks: the sequential learning problem. In: Psychology of Learning and Motivation, vol. 24, pp. 109–165. Elsevier (1989)

18. Paszke, A., et al.: Automatic differentiation in PyTorch. In: Proceedings of the Advances Neural Information Processing Systems Workshop (2017)

19. Prabhu, A., Torr, P.H.S., Dokania, P.K.: GDumb: a simple approach that questions our progress in continual learning. In: Vedaldi, A., Bischof, H., Brox, T., Frahm, J.-M. (eds.) ECCV 2020. LNCS, vol. 12347, pp. 524–540. Springer, Cham (2020). https://doi.org/10.1007/978-3-030-58536-5_31

20. Rebuffi, S.A., Kolesnikov, A., Sperl, G., Lampert, C.H.: iCaRL: incremental classifier and representation learning. In: Proceedings of the IEEE Conference on Computer Vision and Pattern Recognition, July 2017

21. Reynolds, D.A.: Gaussian mixture models. Encycl. Biom. **741**, 659–663 (2009)

22. Russakovsky, O., et al.: ImageNet large scale visual recognition challenge. Int. J. Comput. Vis. **115**(3), 211–252 (2015). https://doi.org/10.1007/s11263-015-0816-y

23. Van Gansbeke, W., Vandenhende, S., Georgoulis, S., Proesmans, M., Van Gool, L.: SCAN: learning to classify images without labels. In: Vedaldi, A., Bischof, H., Brox, T., Frahm, J.-M. (eds.) ECCV 2020. LNCS, vol. 12355, pp. 268–285. Springer, Cham (2020). https://doi.org/10.1007/978-3-030-58607-2_16

24. Welling, M.: Herding dynamical weights to learn. In: Proceedings of the International Conference on Machine Learning, pp. 1121–1128 (2009)

25. Wold, S., Esbensen, K., Geladi, P.: Principal component analysis. Chemom. Intell. Lab. Syst. **2**(1–3), 37–52 (1987)

26. Wu, Y., et al.: Large scale incremental learning. In: Proceedings of the IEEE Conference on Computer Vision and Pattern Recognition, June 2019

27. Zhan, X., Xie, J., Liu, Z., Ong, Y.S., Loy, C.C.: Online deep clustering for unsupervised representation learning, pp. 6688–6697 (2020)

28. Zhao, B., Xiao, X., Gan, G., Zhang, B., Xia, S.T.: Maintaining discrimination and fairness in class incremental learning. In: Proceedings of the IEEE Conference on Computer Vision and Pattern Recognition, pp. 13208–13217 (2020)

Transfer and Continual Supervised Learning for Robotic Grasping Through Grasping Features

Luca Monorchio[1] , Marco Capotondi[2(✉)] , Mario Corsanici[2] ,
Wilson Villa[1] , Alessandro De Luca[2] , and Francesco Puja[1]

[1] Konica Minolta Global R&D Europe, Rome, Italy
{luca.monorchio,wilson.villa,francesco.puja}@konicaminolta.it
[2] DIAG, Sapienza University of Rome, Rome, Italy
{capotondi,corsanici,deluca}@diag.uniroma1.it

Abstract. We present a Transfer and Continual Learning method for robotic grasping tasks, based on small vision-depth (RGBD) datasets and realized through the use of Grasping Features. Given a network architecture composed by a CNN (Convolutional Neural Network) followed by a FCC (Fully Connected Cascade Neural Network), we exploit high-level features specific of the grasping tasks, as extracted by the convolutional network from RGBD images. These features are more descriptive of a grasping task than just visual ones, and thus more efficient for transfer learning purposes. Being datasets for visual grasping less common than those for image recognition, we also propose an efficient way to generate these data using only simple geometric structures. This reduces the computational burden of the FCC and allows to obtain a better performance with the same amount of data. Simulation results using the collaborative UR-10 robot and a jaw gripper are reported to show the quality of the proposed method.

Keywords: Transfer Learning · Continual Learning · Robotic grasping

1 Introduction

Automatic manipulation of objects is one of the main tasks that every robotic system has to accomplish in order to interact with the environment and cooperate with a human. As a generic definition, a grasping task requires a robot manipulator equipped with a gripper and sensors (e.g., a RGB camera and depth sensor) to pick up, move, and place down an object between assigned Cartesian poses in an unstructured environment (see Fig. 1).

This basic problem has been tackled first with analytical methods, mostly using vision and force feedback [8,9]. However, the presence of multiple kinematic and dynamic constraints has limited so far their success, restricting the field of application to particular types of objects in well-defined environments. More recently, following the widespread diffusion of data driven methods for image

F. Cuzzolin et al. (Eds.): CSSL 2021, LNAI 13418, pp. 33–47, 2022.
https://doi.org/10.1007/978-3-031-17587-9_3

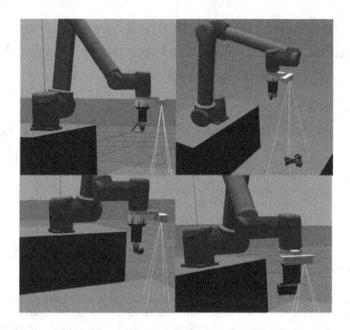

Fig. 1. Snapshots of the simulated UR-10 robot equipped with a jaw gripper performing the grasping procedure on different objects.

processing, the problem has been addressed through Deep Learning (DL) techniques, as in [1]. Within this paradigm, Supervised and Unsupervised Learning and also Reinforcement Learning were used.

Both Supervised and Unsupervised methods are based on classification and regression of the grasping pose, usually parametrized by the Tool Center Point and the approach vector, as assigned to a set of successful previous grasping experiences. In supervised methods, the datasets are generated within a procedure that is independent from the learning process, whereas in unsupervised methods, the same learning algorithm is queried in inference for generating the grasping policy and for producing samples accordingly. On the other hand, Reinforcement Learning realizes the search of a policy for generating either the grasping pose or the entire movement through a mechanism of trials and rewards [13].

In order to improve efficiency and to limit data hungriness of the above learning techniques when applied to several different objects in industrial and human environments, two special DL concepts have been developed for generalization and knowledge storage: Transfer Learning (TL), which consists in the transfer of knowledge from a certain domain or task to another, and Continual Learning (CL), which addresses the storage of previous knowledge after changing the application task [2,12]. Both methods were found to be very useful when implementing learning algorithms in real-world applications, limiting the need of retraining and improving the reuse of acquired knowledge. This is particularly relevant when the data are generated by means of physical trials of robotic manipulation, a procedure that is time consuming and potentially dangerous.

In this paper, we present a method to realize Transfer and Continual Supervised Learning in the context of vision-depth based robotic grasping tasks. Different CL methodologies have been exploited for robotics, as surveyed by [10]. In our work, we focus on regularization-based techniques. In particular, a predefined architecture composed by a Convolutional Neural Network (CNN) followed by a Fully Connected Network (FCC) is used to process RGBD images, and its main properties are exploited so as to become as little data hungry as possible and, at the same time, still completely aware of the task. Differently from [18], we propose here to modify the classical transfer learning procedure by using high-level features that we call Grasping Features (GFs). These are generated from the CNN during the training on a specific grasping task, instead of the visual features generated by training on datasets suited for image recognition and segmentation [16].

The use of Grasping Features introduces many advantages both for Transfer and Continual Learning. In fact, instead of completely decoupling the grasping task from its features, delegating the CNN to visual recognition only and thus forcing the FCC to learn both the grasping task and the variability of the objects to be grasped, the GFs already encode information about the grasping task, allowing the FCC to be fine tuned only for coping with object variety. As a result, this allows the use of smaller sets of data. On the other hand, the main limitation to the use of GFs in TL is that datasets composed by samples of robotic grasping are very uncommon and also quite dependent on the dataset generation policy—as far as we know, the only open dataset for grasping is the one provided by the Cornell University [6].

Because of the restricted availability of data and in order to obtain an efficient implementation of the proposed method, we introduce a strategy for generating larger datasets that uses only grasping of basic objects with simple geometry in a procedure that we call Shape Decomposition. Our claim is that the use of Grasping Features and the generation of a knowledge base through Shape Decomposition allow an efficient pipeline of Continual Learning in cascade to Transfer Learning even with relatively few data. In fact, the use of relevant high-level features in a more informative dataset reduces the training effort of the FCC. Fine tuning on new objects will become easier, with improvement in TL performance, while saturation of the FCC weights will occur later, offering thus more freedom to regularization and preventing catastrophic forgetting events.

The paper is organized as follows. In Sect. 2, we formulate the grasping problem and introduce the basic assumptions of the solution method. In Sect. 3, the learning network architecture is defined, focusing in particular on the dataset generation procedure and on TL and CL issues. The implementation details are described in Sect. 4, while Sect. 5 reports the results obtained in a simulated environment. Conclusions and future work are summarized in Sect. 6.

2 Problem Formulation

We introduce here the formulation of the grasping problem and the main working assumptions underlying our solution method.

While grasping is defined in many ways in the literature, for the sake of this paper we consider the following definition. A grasping task consists in the use of a robotic system to pick up and move a certain class of objects placed on a flat surface, using a gripper and an RGBD camera mounted on the robot end effector. Such definition is technically independent from the type of robot used for the task, depending only on the gripper structure, the grasping policy, the object properties and the camera features.

Real objects have usually very complex shapes with different mechanical properties (such as weight or CoM position), so that the grasping policy cannot be the same for all objects and a specific algorithm for its generation is required. We define the grasping policy as follows. Consider a robot end effector mounting a gripper and carrying a RGBD camera that provides RGB and depth images. The grasping policy consists in an algorithm that provides a Grasping Tuple (GT) $[x, y, \theta]$ corresponding to the desired Cartesian coordinates and orientation of the gripper in the image plane. According to the depth measurements and image coordinates, the GT is transformed into the world frame of the robot. A planner computes a feasible path for the robot end effector, with resulting commands issued in the joint space. The robot will execute the motion from its home position to the desired end-effector pose and will try then to grasp the object, according to the particular structure of the gripper (e.g., with jaws, vacuum suction, or multiple fingers).

With this definition of a grasping task, the problem is now shifted to the regression of the functional map that generates suitable values of the GT. In the following, we will introduce improvements that are valid in principle for any data driven algorithm used to solve the GT regression problem, assuming that RGBD images are processed by a neural network with a particular structure.

3 Network Architecture

We specify here the type of architecture we have considered in our experiments, together with the method of Transfer and Continual Learning we exploit.

With reference to Fig. 2, the network architecture for solving the GT regression problem is composed by a Convolutional Neural Network (CNN), that takes as input the stack of RGB and depth images provided by the camera, and by a Fully Connected Cascade Neural Network (FCC), that takes as input the output of the CNN, returning the predicted Grasping Tuple as output.

It is well known that CNNs are able to pre-process efficiently images, extracting high-level features of images such as vertices, angles, shapes, or color [3]. In our architecture, the CNN goal is still to encode the high-dimensional image input to a low-dimensional output for the cascaded processing by the FCC, but we let the CNN produce an intermediate output that eases the FCC task of generating the desired grasp.

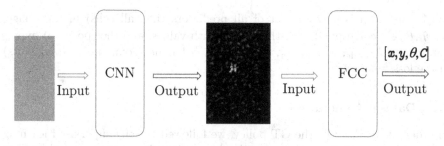

Fig. 2. Scheme of a generic network architecture, in which image pre-processing is executed by the CNN and fed as input to the FCC that returns as the Grasping Tuple (including the confidence level C) as output.

For this, we use as starting point the network described in [11], on top which we build the entire TL-CL pipeline. This architecture is structurally similar to the YOLO introduced by [15], but with a different goal. It takes as input RGBD images and returns as output a series of Grasping Tuples (GTs) stacked with their confidence level, a value that quantifies how much the network is confident about the returned prediction. The input images are divided in cells, each associated to a specific prediction and centered in different image coordinates. The architecture returns as output a tuple composed by the relative position of the gripper (x, y) with respect to the cell, its absolute orientation θ, and the associated confidence C. The Grasping Tuple is thus redefined as $[x, y, \theta, C]$ and the addition of confidence values in the output modifies slightly the regression. For the robot grasping, the relative positions predicted by the network are transformed in world positions according to the RGBD measurements.

While in YOLO proposals are pruned according to the predicted probability of the single bounding box, in our structure all predictions are considered individually and sorted by increasing confidence. Keeping more proposals is not a drawback in general, since in many industrial cases multiple grasps are acceptable (or convenient) –a typical example is the task of emptying bins from a container.

The supervised learning procedure minimizes a loss function L_task which is the weighted sum of quadratic terms, one for each component of the tuple, corresponding to the squared difference between network prediction and ground truth:

$$L_\text{task} = \lambda_\text{position} \sum_{i=0}^{S^2} [(x_i - \hat{x}_i)^2 + (y_i - \hat{y}_i)^2)]$$
$$+ \lambda_\text{orientation} \sum_{i=0}^{S^2} (\theta_i - \hat{\theta}_i)^2 + \lambda_\text{confidence} \sum_{i=0}^{S^2} (C_i - \hat{C}_i)^2. \tag{1}$$

In (1), the sum is over the set of all predictors (i.e., all cells) in the image, $[\hat{x}_i, \hat{y}_i, \hat{\theta}_i, \hat{C}_i]$ corresponds to i-th ground truth values, and the (positive) hyper-parameters λ_{coords}, $\lambda_{\text{orientation}}$, and $\lambda_{\text{confidence}}$ balance components (and units) in the loss function.

3.1   Dataset Generation

In order to correctly fit the GT policy, we followed a (self) supervised learning approach, automatically generating the dataset in a decoupled way with respect to the training procedure. Consider an input RGBD image specified by

$$X \in R^4 \times R^{\text{P}},$$

with the R, G, B, and D data of a camera having a total of P pixels, and a tuple

$$Y = [x, y, \theta, C],$$

where x and y correspond to the Cartesian coordinates of the grasping position in the image reference, θ is the roll angle of the gripper, and C is the confidence value, a real number in $[0, 1]$. The regression problem corresponds to approximating the map

$$f : X \to Y.$$

In order to collect samples of this map, a quasi-random policy is employed, with a bounding box generated around the object using selective search algorithms [17] and grasping positions randomly picked inside the box. As for the gripper orientation, a random value is drawn from the interval $(-\pi, \pi]$. For each proposed GT, a grasping trial is executed, associating $C = 1$ in case of successful grasping and $C = 0$ otherwise. All (positive and negative) trials are stacked in the dataset used for network training.

3.2   Supervised Transfer and Continual Learning

For effective human-robot interaction and in industrial applications, scalability of the approach with respect to the increasing cardinality of the set of objects considered in the grasping task is an appealing property. Techniques for Transfer and Continual Learning have been exploited in order to avoid redundant training and allow the largest possible reuse of previous knowledge.

In particular, in our TL procedure for grasping, we trained first the entire network on a large set of objects having different shapes and structural properties (Baseline Training). Afterwards, in order to realize a fine tuning on unknown new objects, we trained again the FCC while keeping the previously obtained weights of the CNN fixed. The main idea of this approach is similar to what was realized for pure visual tasks [4]. In the context of grasping, this approach has been exploited by [18].

Moreover, among the many existing CL approaches [10], we resorted to a regularization of the FCC weights, according to our idea that the two different components of the network, CNN and FCC, are delegated to TL and CL, respectively.

In this context, the goal of CL is to solve multiple learning tasks in such way that the overall network, after training on new objects, preserves still an acceptable level of performance on previous grasping tasks. Regularization is achieved by introducing soft constraints in the optimization, augmenting the loss function in (1) with a weighted distance to previous tasks parameters:

$$L = L_{\text{task}} + \lambda_{\text{reg}} \overset{\text{previous tasks}}{\sum_{j}} (\mathbf{p} - \mathbf{p}_j)^T \mathbf{W}_j (\mathbf{p} - \mathbf{p}_j). \tag{2}$$

In (2), vectors $\mathbf{p}$ and $\mathbf{p}_j$ are, respectively, the actual and the j-th task weights of the FCC, $\mathbf{W}_j > 0$ is a weight matrix associated to the distance from the j-th task, and the hyper-parameter $\lambda_{\text{reg}} > 0$ balances the regularization term in the total loss.

4   Implementation

We provide here some details on the proposed method, in particular how grasping features differ from visual ones and the rationale of Shape Decomposition.

4.1   Grasping Features

One of the main properties of CNN image pre-processing is the partial explainability of the obtained features after the network filtering and elaboration [20]. Visualization of the network outputs can be very expressive about how the algorithm analyzes and processes images [19]. These concepts are very important for the heuristic justification of transfer learning approaches. As shown by [14], features extracted by a CNN trained on large datasets (such as ImageNet) improve generalization, allowing network adaptation to new objects by retraining only the FCC weights.

In contrast to image processing (such as segmentation or classification) intended only for vision goals, we have added the use of Grasping Features resulting in a different output of the CNN. We illustrate this explicitly in Figs. 3 and 4. A visual comparison is shown between the features extracted by the CNN of a YOLO network, trained only for image recognition and classification, and the GFs extracted by the modified architecture proposed in Sect. 3.

In both the considered situations, namely with a set of real objects and with a single simulated object with noise, the features extracted by the two approaches are quite different. In fact, while the output of the CNN activation functions for image recognition just extract object shapes, the GFs obtained by the CNN trained for grasping show peaks at image points which are more suitable for the task.

Since the Grasping Features embed not only geometric information but also physical properties (such as mass, CoM position and inertia) of the object, they are more informative for the goal of the algorithm. Having a richer input available for the FCC, the same amount of data will induce a faster convergence of its fine tuning. As an expected result, transfer learning is executed with fewer samples (in the order of thousands, instead of millions).

4.2 Shape Decomposition

The use of large datasets of images allows to decouple image pre-processing from grasping policy learning, as realized, e.g., in [18] where all the effort is delegated to the subsequent FCC. Despite the better adherence of Grasping Features to the task allows to distribute the computational burden between CNN and FCC, the main limitation of their application is the scarce availability of grasping datasets. As a matter of fact, GFs reduce but do not eliminate the need of large sets of samples for transfer learning.

We propose to face this issue by generating grasping samples in a convenient mode. Usually, objects encountered in real environments may be decomposed into simpler geometrical shapes, such as spheres, cylinders, or boxes, some of which dominates over the others from the point of view of size and/or physical properties. Figure 5 illustrates visually such concept.

The use of these basic objects improves the efficiency of the dataset. In fact, it is more convenient to approximate the grasping of complex objects as nonlinear combinations (via the FCC) of grasping features extracted from simpler objects rather than vice versa. This is particularly evident in the case of small datasets.

Instead of extracting the correct grasping features from general images using the strength of a large dataset, we decided to use a smaller set of samples but with basic shapes that are similar to the features we expect to extract from the network. Such use of a reduced dataset appears opposite to the general trend in deep learning image-based approaches. Nonetheless, this turned out to be a

Fig. 3. From left to right: Input image of a set of real objects, the visual features extracted from the CNN of a YOLO network, and the associated Grasping Features. The GFs have intensity peaks at the image points of possible grasp positions, while visual features recover just object shapes.

Fig. 4. From left to right: Noisy input image of a simulated hammer, the visual features extracted from the CNN of a YOLO network, and the associated Grasping Features. In the presence of a single object, the GFs have even more distinctive peaks at the image points corresponding to possible grasp positions (in this case the upper part of the hammer). The multiple smaller peaks are due to unfiltered noise.

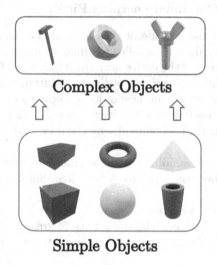

Fig. 5. Shape decomposition: simple objects may be combined to generate complex objects.

Fig. 6. Example of a bolt obtained as the overlap of simpler shapes such as cube and torus.

practical and successful procedure both for TL and CL. In particular, it allows to realize an efficient Continual Learning through regularization methods.

Indeed, random high-level features fed in input to a large FCC network can still be combined in order to approximate the grasping policy for any single object. However, when learning over time the grasp for multiple objects, the regularization process would become almost useless. Because of the low significance of the provided features, the positions in the parameter space of the individual minima of the loss function (1) and of the regularization component in Eq. 2 are in general very separated, thus leading to a spurious solution of the optimization problem. The results in the next section support empirically the validity of our approach.

5   Results

We present here results of numerical tests obtained with a Gazebo simulator, using a 6-dof UR-10 robot equipped with a jaw gripper.

5.1   Transfer and Continual Learning Pipeline

The test pipeline with the cascade of transfer and continual learning is shown in Fig. 7. The test procedure is as follows. First, we use a previously generated baseline dataset for training the entire network (CNN and FCC) so as to extract Grasping Features. Then, the weights of the convolutional layers are frozen and the FCC is trained sequentially on new objects, applying on each new training a regularization with respect to previous items—see Eq. (2). The classification of objects as new or old is realized manually by the user, and datasets are provided accordingly.

For this, we used very small datasets, around 1000 samples for each object (a very small figure when compared to classical transfer learning and fine tuning approaches).

The final system has been tested on a simulated scenario containing all the objects previously encountered. The robot tries to grasp each of the objects and performance is evaluated according to the relative frequency of positive results.

5.2   Simulated Tests

The tests were realized using a set of 11 objects, divided in simple objects (bar, sphere, triangle, cylinder, box, T-shape) and complex objects (hammer, modified T-shape, modified box, cup, scissor), see also Fig. 8. For grasping, the robot uses a very common parallel gripper with two jaws to hold a workpiece.

The Continual Learning procedure is implemented according to [7], as modified by [5]: regularization is performed using only the weights of the last task, the regularization weight is itself a weighted sum of the Fisher matrices of all previous tasks. As for the training algorithm, we used Adam optimizer with a starting learning rate of 0.001, parameters $\beta_1 = 0.9$ and $\beta_2 = 0.999$, a batch size of 4 images, 15 epochs for the baseline training, and 7 epochs for the cascade of regularized training.

Shape Decomposition

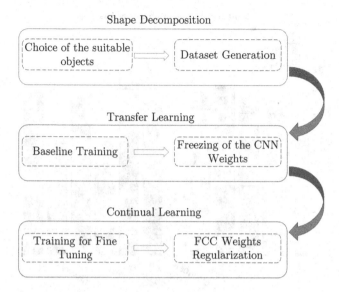

Fig. 7. Pipeline to evaluate the proposed approach for realizing Transfer and Continual Learning.

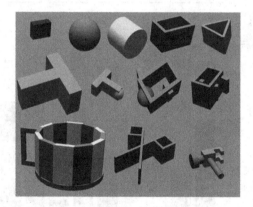

Fig. 8. Different views and scales of the objects used for the tests. The first row shows simple objects, while complex/combined objects are shown in increasing complexity in the second and third rows.

We define the score of the algorithm for each object as the frequency of times (normalized to 1) that the robot successfully grasps the object. Since our architecture generates N predictions for the N cells in the image, we considered in each trial the first 4 grasp proposals with the highest confidence levels. Accordingly, a positive outcome is recorded when at least one of these grasps is successful.

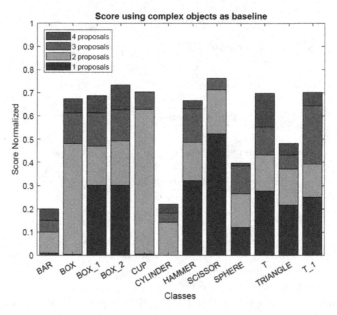

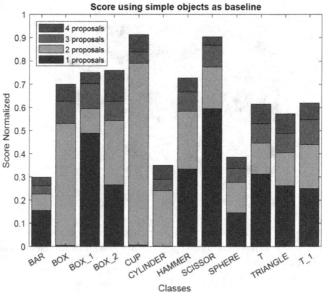

Fig. 9. Performance histograms for different baseline datasets: Using complex objects (top) and using simple objects (bottom). Color codes are used to specify the number of grasp proposals (GTs) used in each trial.

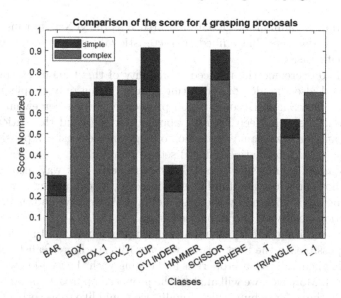

Fig. 10. The histogram compares the scores in the two cases comparison using all 4 grasp proposals in the trials. Improvement using as baseline simple objects for Transfer and Continual learning is evident.

We compared two learning strategies, see Fig. 9. In the first one, we used complex objects for the baseline training and then regularized training on the simple objects, in the same order as they have been listed above. The results in the top histogram of Fig. 9 show that the performance is acceptable despite the few training data, except for some degradation on certain objects (in particular, the bar and the cylinder). Each column in the histogram includes the outcome using partial ordered subsets or the totality of the 4 grasp proposals. In the second strategy, we switched to simple objects for baseline training and complex ones for the regularization, again in the same order as before. The performance is globally improved (center histogram in Fig. 10), and the degradation for the same previous objects is reduced. The last histogram compares the scores of the two strategies, considering for each object all 4 grasp proposals in the trials.

Summarizing, both strategies give a merit to the benefit of using Grasping Features in order to reduce the size of the training dataset. Moreover, the final score is improved when the baseline dataset is composed by simple objects, according to the Shape Decomposition idea, followed by the use of complex objects in the CL pipeline.

6   Conclusions

We have presented an original method for realizing Transfer Learning (TL) and Continual Learning (CL) for RGBD-based robotic grasping tasks. The basic idea is to define a more efficient transfer learning not using just visual features extracted from a common image databases (such as ImageNet) but instead with grasp-oriented datasets that embed characteristic Grasping Features extracted for the specific tasks.

In order to overcome the reduced availability of this type of grasping data, we introduced also the idea of generating samples using only simple geometric shapes through a Shape Decomposition procedure. This is somewhat opposite to the current trend in deep learning approaches: we avoid the critical (time-consuming and/or hazardous) generation of huge datasets using a physical robot by providing more informative reduced sets of samples.

Our obtained results show that TL is possible in this way also with very few data (thousands instead of millions). Moreover, by comparing how much the TL+CL pipeline is affected by the baseline dataset, we have shown that Shape Decomposition positively affects performance.

Though promising, these results are indeed preliminary and many improvements are possible. In the next future, we plan to use a more realistic simulator for improving generalization properties and coping with the well-known problem of SimToReal. Moreover, we will analyse the proposed approach for larger classes of objects (in the order of hundreds). Finally, we would like to use other CL methods, to highlight how much the Grasping Features and the Shape Decomposition are adaptable to different algorithms.

References

1. Bohg, J., Morales, A., Asfour, T., Kragic, D.: Data-driven grasp synthesis-a survey. IEEE Trans. Robot. **30**(2), 289–309 (2014). https://doi.org/10.1109/TRO.2013.2289018
2. Delange, M., et al.: A continual learning survey: defying forgetting in classification tasks. IEEE Trans. Pattern Anal. Mach. Intell. **44**(7), 3366–3385 (2022). https://doi.org/10.1109/TPAMI.2021.3057446
3. Goodfellow, I., Bengio, Y., Courville, A.: Deep Learning. MIT Press (2016). http://www.deeplearningbook.org
4. Huh, M., Agrawal, P., Efros, A.A.: What makes ImageNet good for transfer learning? CoRR abs/1608.08614 (2016). http://arxiv.org/abs/1608.08614
5. Huszár, F.: Note on the quadratic penalties in elastic weight consolidation. Proc. Natl. Acad. Sci. **115**(11), E2496–E2497 (2018). https://doi.org/10.1073/pnas.1717042115. https://www.pnas.org/content/115/11/E2496
6. Jiang, Y., Moseson, S., Saxena, A.: Efficient grasping from RGBD images: learning using a new rectangle representation. In: Proceedings of IEEE International Conference on Robotics and Automation, pp. 3304–3311 (2011). https://doi.org/10.1109/ICRA.2011.5980145
7. Kirkpatrick, J., et al.: Overcoming catastrophic forgetting in neural networks. Proc. Natl. Acad. Sci. **114**(13), 3521–3526 (2017). https://doi.org/10.1073/pnas.1611835114. https://www.pnas.org/content/114/13/3521
8. Kragic, D., Daniilidis, K.: 3-D vision for navigation and grasping. In: Siciliano, B., Khatib, O. (eds.) Springer Handbook of Robotics, pp. 811–824. Springer, Cham (2016). https://doi.org/10.1007/978-3-319-32552-1_32

9. Kuffner, J., Xiao, J.: Motion for manipulation tasks. In: Siciliano, B., Khatib, O. (eds.) Springer Handbook of Robotics, pp. 897–930. Springer, Cham (2016). https://doi.org/10.1007/978-3-319-32552-1_36

10. Lesort, T., Lomonaco, V., Stoian, A., Maltoni, D., Filliat, D., Díaz-Rodríguez, N.: Continual learning for robotics: definition, framework, learning strategies, opportunities and challenges. Inf. Fusion **58**, 52–68 (2020). https://doi.org/10.1016/j.inffus.2019.12.004. https://www.sciencedirect.com/science/article/pii/S1566253519307377

11. Monorchio, L., Evangelista, D., Imperoli, M., Pretto, A.: Learning from successes and failures to grasp objects with a vacuum gripper. In: IEEE/RSJ IROS Workshop on Task-Informed Grasping for Rigid and Deformable Object Manipulation (2018)

12. Pan, S.J., Yang, Q.: A survey on transfer learning. IEEE Trans. Knowl. Data Eng. **22**(10), 1345–1359 (2010). https://doi.org/10.1109/TKDE.2009.191

13. Quillen, D., Jang, E., Nachum, O., Finn, C., Ibarz, J., Levine, S.: Deep reinforcement learning for vision-based robotic grasping: a simulated comparative evaluation of off-policy methods. In: Proceedings of IEEE International Conference on Robotics and Automation, pp. 6284–6291 (2018). https://doi.org/10.1109/ICRA.2018.8461039

14. Razavian, A.S., Azizpour, H., Sullivan, J., Carlsson, S.: CNN features off-the-shelf: an astounding baseline for recognition. In: Proceedings of IEEE Conference on Computer Vision and Pattern Recognition Workshops, pp. 512–519 (2014)

15. Redmon, J., Divvala, S., Girshick, R., Farhadi, A.: You only look once: unified, real-time object detection. In: 2016 IEEE Conference on Computer Vision and Pattern Recognition, pp. 779–788 (2016). https://doi.org/10.1109/CVPR.2016.91

16. Saxena, A., Driemeyer, J., Ng, A.Y.: Robotic grasping of novel objects using vision. Int. J. Robot. Res. **27**(2), 157–173 (2008). https://doi.org/10.1177/0278364907087172

17. Uijlings, J.R.R., van de Sande, K.E.A., Gevers, T., et al.: Selective search for object recognition. Int. J. Comput. Vis. **104**(2), 154–171 (2013). https://doi.org/10.1007/s11263-013-0620-5

18. Yen-Chen, L., Zeng, A., Song, S., Isola, P., Lin, T.Y.: Learning to see before learning to act: visual pre-training for manipulation. In: Proceedings of IEEE International Conference on Robotics and Automation, pp. 7286–7293 (2020). https://doi.org/10.1109/ICRA40945.2020.9197331

19. Zeiler, M.D., Fergus, R.: Visualizing and understanding convolutional networks. CoRR abs/1311.2901 (2013). http://arxiv.org/abs/1311.2901

20. Zhang, Q., Wu, Y.N., Zhu, S.C.: Interpretable convolutional neural networks. In: Proceedings of IEEE/CVF Conference on Computer Vision and Pattern Recognition, pp. 8827–8836 (2018). https://doi.org/10.1109/CVPR.2018.00920

Unsupervised Continual Learning via Self-adaptive Deep Clustering Approach

Mahardhika Pratama[1]([✉])(ID), Andri Ashfahani[2], and Edwin Lughofer[3]

[1] STEM, University of South Australia, Adelaide, Australia
dhika.pratama@unisa.edu.au
[2] SCSE, Nanyang Technological University, Singapore, Singapore
andriash001@e.ntu.edu.sg
[3] DKBMS, Johanes Kepler University, Linz, Austria
edwin.lughofer@jku.at

Abstract. Unsupervised continual learning remains a relatively uncharted territory in the existing literature because the vast majority of existing works call for unlimited access of ground truth incurring expensive labelling cost. Another issue lies in the problem of task boundaries and task IDs which must be known for model's updates or model's predictions hindering feasibility for real-time deployment. Knowledge Retention in Self-Adaptive Deep Continual Learner, (KIERA), is proposed in this paper. KIERA is developed from the notion of flexible deep clustering approach possessing an elastic network structure to cope with changing environments in the timely manner. The centroid-based experience replay is put forward to overcome the catastrophic forgetting problem. KIERA does not exploit any labelled samples for model updates while featuring a task-agnostic merit. The advantage of KIERA has been numerically validated in popular continual learning problems where it shows highly competitive performance compared to state-of-the art approaches. Our implementation is available in https://researchdata. ntu.edu.sg/dataset.xhtml?persistentId=doi:10.21979/N9/P9DFJH.

Keywords: Continual learning · Lifelong learning · Unsupervised learning

1 Introduction

Continual learning is a machine learning field studying a learning model which can handle a sequence of tasks $T_1, T_2, T_3, ..., T_K$ [12] where K labels the number of tasks. Unlike conventional learning problem with the i.i.d assumption, every task T_k suffers from non-stationary conditions where there exists drifting data

M. Pratama and A. Ashfahani share equal contributions. This work was carried out when M. Pratama was with SCSE, NTU, Singapore.

distributions $P(X,Y)_k \neq P(X,Y)_{k+1}$, emergence of new classes or combination between both conditions. The goal of general continual learning should be to build a model $f(.)$ which is capable of identifying and adapting to changes without suffering from the catastrophic forgetting problem. It is done on the fly with the absence of samples from previous tasks T_{k-1}.

There has been growing research interest in the continual learning domain in which the main goal is to resolve the issue of catastrophic forgetting thereby actualizing knowledge retention property of a model. These works can be divided into three categories: memory-based approach, regularization-based approach and structure-based approach. **Memory-based Approach** is designed to handle the continual learning problem with the use of external memory storing past samples. Past samples are replayed along with new samples of the current task such that the catastrophic forgetting problem can be addressed. **Regularization-based approach** is put forward with the use of additional regularization term in the cost function aiming at achieving tradeoff points between old task and new task. **Structure-based approach** is developed under the roof of dynamic structure. It adds new network components to cope with new tasks while isolating old parameters from new task to avoid the catastrophic forgetting problem.

The area of continual learning still deserves in-depth study because the vast majority of existing approaches are fully-supervised algorithms limiting their applications in the scarcity of labelled samples. Existing approaches rely on a very strong assumption of task boundaries and task IDs. This assumption is impractical because the point of changes is often unknown and the presence of task IDs for inference imply extra domain knowledge.

An unsupervised continual learning algorithm, namely Knowledge Retention in Self-Adaptive Deep Continual Learner (KIERA), is proposed in this paper. KIERA does not utilize any labelled samples for model updates. That is, labelled samples are only offered to establish clusters-to-classes associations required to perform classification tasks. KIERA is constructed from the idea of self-evolving deep clustering network making use of a different-depth network structure. Every hidden layer generates its own set of clusters and produces its own local outputs. This strategy enables an independent self-evolving clustering mechanism to be performed in different levels of deep embedding spaces. KIERA features an elastic network structure in which its hidden nodes, layers and clusters are self-generated from data streams in respect to varying data distributions.

The parameter learning mechanism of KIERA is devised to achieve a clustering-friendly latent space via simultaneous feature learning and clustering. It puts forward reconstruction loss and clustering loss minimized simultaneously in the framework of stacked autoencoder (SAE) to avoid trivial solutions. The clustering loss is formed as the K-Means loss [19] inducing the clustering-friendly latent space where data samples are forced to be adjacent to the winning cluster, i.e., the most neighboring cluster to a data sample. The centroid-based experience replay strategy is put forward to address the catastrophic interference problem. That is, the sample selection mechanism is carried out in respect to focal-points, i.e., data samples triggering addition of clusters. The selective sampling mechanism is integrated to assure a bounded replay buffer. This component also differs

KIERA from our earlier work, ADCN [2], where the LWF-like regularization strategy [8] is applied to combat the catastrophic forgetting problem. The advantage of KIERA is confirmed with rigorous numerical study in popular problems where it outperforms prominent algorithms.

This paper presents four major contributions: 1) KIERA is proposed to handle unsupervised continual learning problems; 2) the flexible deep clustering approach is put forward in which hidden layers, nodes and clusters are self-evolved on the fly; 3) the different-depth network structure is designed making possible an independent clustering module to be carried out in different levels of deep embedding space; 4) the centroid-based experience replay method is put forward to address the catastrophic interference problem.

2   Related Works

Memory-Based Approach: iCaRL [14] exemplifies the memory-based approach in the continual learning using the exemplar set of each class. The classification decision is calculated from the similarity degree of a new sample to the exemplar set. Another example of the memory-based approach is Gradient Episodic Memory (GEM) [9] where past samples are stored to calculate the forgetting case. A forgetting case can be examined from the angle between the gradient vector and the proposed update. This work is extended in [3] and called Averaged GEM (AGEM). Its contribution lies in the modification of the loss function to expedite the model updates. Deep Generative Replay (DGR) [17] does not utilize external memory to address the catastrophic forgetting problem rather makes use of generative adversarial network (GAN) to create representation of old tasks. The catastrophic forgetting is addressed by generating pseudo samples for experience replay mechanism. Our work is framed under this category, because it can be executed without the presence of task IDs or task's boundaries.

Regularization-Based Approach: Elastic Weight Consolidation (EWC) [6] is a prominent regularization-based approach using the L2-like regularization approach constraining the movement of important network parameters. It constructs Fisher Information Matrix (FIM) to signify the importance of network parameters. Synaptic Intelligence (SI) [21] offers an alternative approach where it utilizes accumulated gradients to quantify importance of network importance instead of FIM incurring prohibitive computational burdens. Memory Aware Synapses (MAS) [1] is an EWC-like approach with modification of parameter importance matrix using an unsupervised and online criterion. EWC has been extended in [16] named online EWC where Laplace approximation is put forward to construct the parameter importance matrix. Learning Without Forgetting (LWF) is proposed in [8] where it formulates a joint optimization problem between the current loss function and the knowledge distillation loss [5]. This neuron-based regularization notion is presented in [11] where the regularization is performed by adjusting the learning rates of stochastic gradient descent. In [10], the inter-task synaptic mapping is proposed. Notwithstanding that the regularization-based approach is computationally efficient, this approach requires the task boundaries and task IDs to be known.

Structure-Based Approach: The catastrophic forgetting is overcome in progressive neural networks (PNNs) [15] by introduction of new column for every new task while freezing old network parameters. This approach is, however, not scalable for large-scale problem since the structural complexity linearly grows as the number of tasks. This drawback is addressed in [20] with the use of selective retraining approach. Learn-to-grow is proposed in [7] where it utilizes the neural architecture search to find the best network structure of a given task. The structure-based approach imposes expensive complexities.

3   Problem Formulation

The continual learning problem aims to build a predictive model $f(.)$ handling streaming tasks $T_1, T_2, T_3, ..., T_K$ where K denotes the number of tasks. Unlike conventional problems assuming the i.i.d condition, each task T_k is influenced by non-stationary conditions. There exist two types of changes in the continual learning where the first one is known as the problem of changing data distributions while the second one is understood as the problem of changing target classes. The problem of changing data distributions or the concept drift problem is defined as a change of joint probability distribution $P(X, Y)_k \neq P(X, Y)_{k+1}$. The problem of changing target classes refers to different target classes of each task. Suppose that L_k and $L_{k'}$ stand for the label sets of the $k - th$ task and the $k' - th$ task, $\forall k, k' L_k \cap L_{k'} = \emptyset$ for $k \neq k'$. This problem is also known as the incremental class problem. Each task normally consists of paired data samples $T_k = \{x_n, y_n\}_{n=1}^{N_k}$ where N_k denotes the size of the $k - th$ task. $x_n \in \Re^{u \times u}$ is the $n - th$ input image while $y_n \in \{l_1, l_2, ..., l_m\}$ is the target vector formed as a one-hot vector. This assumption, however, does not apply in the unsupervised continual learning dealing with the scarcity of labelled samples. The access of true class labels is only provided for the initial batch of each task to associate the cluster's centroids with classes $B_0^k = \{x_n, y_n\}_{n=1}^{N_0^k}$ while the remainder of data samples arrive with the absence of labelled samples $B_j^k = \{x_n\}_{n=1}^{N_j^k}$. Note that $N_0^k + N_1^k + N_j^k ... + N_j^k = N_k$.

4   Learning Policy of KIERA

4.1   Network Structure

KIERA is structured as a SAE comprising two components: feature extraction layer and fully-connected layer. The feature extraction layer is built upon a convolutional layer or a nonlinear layer. It maps an input image x into a latent input vector $Z \in \Re^{u'}$ where u' denotes the number of natural features. The fully connected layer performs the encoding and decoding steps across L_{sae} layers producing a reconstructed latent input vector $\hat{Z}$. The reconstructed latent input vector $\hat{Z}$ is further fed to transposed convolutional or nonlinear layers generating the reconstructed input image $\hat{x}$.

Suppose that $h^{l-1} \in \Re^{u_l}$ stands for the latent input vector of the $l - th$ encoder where $h^0 = Z$, the encoder projects h^{l-1} to a lower dimensional latent space $h^l = r(W_{enc}^l h^{l-1} + b_l)$ while the decoder reconstructs the latent input vector $\hat{h}^{l-1} = r(W_{dec}^l + c_l)$. $r(.)$ is a ReLU activation function inducing a nonlinear mapping. $W_{enc}^l \in \Re^{R_l \times u_l}, b_l \in \Re^{R_l}$ are the connective weight and bias of the $l - th$ encoder while $W_{dec}^l \in \Re^{u_l \times R_l}, c_l \in \Re^{u_l}$ are the connective weight and bias of the $l - th$ decoder. R_l, u_l are respectively the number of hidden nodes of the $l - th$ layer and the number of input features of the $l - th$ layer. The tied-weight constraint is applied here to avoid the over-training problem $W_{enc}^l = (W_{dec}^l)^T$. The SAE carries out the non-linear dimension reduction step preventing the trivial solution as the case of the linear dimension reduction mechanism while the training process occurs in the greedy layer-wise fashion.

The unique facet of KIERA lies in the different-depth network structure in which the clustering mechanism takes place in every hidden layer of the fully connected layer $h^l(.)$ thereby producing its own local output. It distinguishes itself from the conventional deep clustering network where the clustering mechanism happens at the bottleneck layer only [19]. The cluster's allegiance is expressed:

$$ale_{s,l} = \frac{\exp\left(-||C_{s,l} - h_l||\right)}{\max_{s=1,\ldots,Cls_l} \exp\left(-||C_{s,l} - h_l||\right)} \tag{1}$$

where $C_{s,l}$ denotes the centroid of the $s - th$ cluster of the $l - th$ layer and Cls_l stands for the number of clusters of the $l - th$ layer. The cluster's allegiance [18] is averaged across all labelled samples $B_0^k = \{x_i, y_i\}_{n=1}^{N_0^k}$ to indicate cluster's tendency to a target class. Let $N_0^{k,o}$ be the number of initially labelled samples of the $k - th$ task falling into the $o - th$ target class where $N_0^{k,1} + N_0^{k,o} + \ldots + N_0^{k,m} = N_0^k$, the averaged cluster allegiance is written:

$$Ale_{s,l}^o = \frac{\sum_{n=1}^{N_0^{k,o}} ale_{s,l}^{n,o}}{N_0^{k,o}} \tag{2}$$

(2) implies a low cluster allegiance of unclean clusters being populated by data samples of mixed classes. The score of the $o - th$ target class of the $l - th$ layer is computed by combining the cluster's allegiance and the distance to a data sample h^l:

$$Score_o^l = Softmax(\sum_{s=1}^{Cls_l} \exp\left(-||h_l - C_{s,l}||\right) Ale_{s,l}^o) \tag{3}$$

The local output of the $l - th$ layer can be found by taking a maximum operation $\max_{o=1,\ldots,m} Score_o^l$. The use of $Softmax(.)$ operation assures the partition of unity as well as the uniform range of $Score_o^l$ across L_{sae} layers. The final output is produced by aggregating the local outputs using the summation operation as follows:

$$\hat{y} = \arg \max_{o=1,\dots,m} \sum_{l=1}^{L_{sae}} Score_o^l \qquad (4)$$

Labelled samples of each task B_0^k are only exploited to associate a cluster to a specific class, i.e., the calculation of cluster allegiance (2) without any labelled samples for model updates. Another typical characteristic of KIERA exists in its self-evolving property where R_l, L_{sae}, Cls_l are not deterministic rather self-evolved from data streams.

4.2 Structural Learning Mechanism

Evolution of Hidden Nodes: KIERA features an elastic network width where new nodes are dynamically added while inactive nodes are pruned. This strategy is underpinned by the network significance (NS) method [13] estimating the generalization power of a network based on the bias and variance decomposition approach. New nodes are introduced in the case of high bias to cope with the underfitting issue while inconsequential nodes are discarded in the case of high variance to overcome the overfitting situation. Because of the absence of any labelled samples for model's updates, the network bias and variance are estimated from reconstructions losses of a layer $NS = Bias^2 + Var = (E[\hat{h}_l] - h_l)^2 + (E[\hat{h}_l^2] - E[\hat{h}_l]^2)$. Note that KIERA adopts the greedy layer-wise training approach. The network bias and variance are formalized under a normal distribution $p(x) = N(\mu, \sigma^2)$ and the RelU activation function $r(.)$ where μ, σ^2 are the mean and standard deviation of data samples. The modified statistical process control (SPC) method [4], a popular approach for anomaly detection, is utilized to signal the high bias condition and the high variance condition as follows:

$$\mu_{bias}^n + \sigma_{bias}^n \geq \mu_{bias}^{min} + (\ln(l) + 1) \times k_1 \sigma_{bias}^{min} \qquad (5)$$

$$\mu_{var}^n + \sigma_{var}^n \geq \mu_{var}^{min} + 2 \times (\ln(l) + 1) \times k_2 \sigma_{var}^{min} \qquad (6)$$

where the main modification of the conventional SPC lies in $k_1 = 1.3 \exp(-Bias^2) + 0.7$ and $k_2 = 1.3 \exp(-Var^2) + 0.7$ leading to dynamic confidence levels. This idea enables new nodes to be crafted in the case of high bias and inconsequential nodes to be removed in the case of high variance. The Xavier's initialization approach is applied for the sake of initialization. Conversely, the pruning process targets an inactive node having the least statistical contribution $\min_{i=1,\dots,R_l} E[\hat{h}_i^l]$. The term $(\ln(l) + 1)$ is inserted to guarantee the nonlinear feature reduction step due to $R_l < R_{l-1}$. The node growing strategy becomes insensitive as the increase of network depth. The term 2 is applied in (6) to prevent a new node to be directly eliminated.

Evolution of Hidden Layer: KIERA characterizes a variable network depth where a drift detection technique is applied to expand the network depth L_{sae}. A new layer is incorporated if a drift is detected. Note that insertion of a new layer is capable of boosting the network's capacity more significantly than that introduction of new nodes. Since no labelled samples are available at all, the drift detection mechanism focuses on the dynamic of latent input features Z extracted by the feature extraction layer. Nevertheless, the characteristic of latent input features are insensitive to changing data distributions. We apply the drift detection method for the last two consecutive data batches $A = [Z_{j-1}^k, Z_j^k]$ here. The drift detection mechanism first finds a cutting point cut signifying the increase of population means $\hat{A} + \epsilon_A \leq \hat{B} + \epsilon_B$. $\hat{A}, \hat{B}$ are the statistics of two data matrices $A \in \Re^{2N_j^k \times u'}$ and $B \in \Re^{cut \times u'}$ respectively while $\epsilon_{A,B} = \sqrt{\frac{1}{2 \times size} \ln \frac{1}{\alpha}}$ is their corresponding Hoeffding's bounds and α is the significance level. $size$ is the size of data matrix of interest.

Once finding the cutting point, the data matrix A is divided into two matrices B and $C^{(2N_j^k - cut) \times u'}$. A drift is confirmed if $|B - C| \geq \epsilon_d$ whereas a warning is flagged by $\epsilon_d \geq |B - C| \geq \epsilon_w$. $\epsilon_{d,w} = (b - a) \sqrt{\frac{(size - cut)}{2 * size * cut} \ln \frac{1}{\alpha_{d,w}}}$ where $[a, b]$ represents the interval of the data matrix A and $\alpha_d < \alpha_w$. The warning condition is a transition situation where the drift condition is to be confirmed by a next stream. A new layer is added if a drift condition is signalled where its nodes are set at the half of that of the previous layer to induce feature reduction. Addition of a new layer does not impose the catastrophic forgetting because of the different-depth network structure, i.e., every layer produces its local output.

Evolution of Hidden Clusters: The growing strategy of hidden clusters relies on the compatibility measure examining a distance between a latent sample h^l to the nearest cluster. A new cluster is added if a data sample is deemed remote to the zone of influence of any existing clusters as follows:

$$\min_{s=1,...,Cls_l} D(C_{s,l}, h^l) > \mu_{D_{s,l}} + k_3 * \sigma_{D_{s,l}} \tag{7}$$

where $\mu_{D_{s,l}}, \sigma_{D_{s,l}}$ are the mean and standard deviation of the distance measure $D(C_{s,l}, h^l)$ while $k_3 = 2 \exp -||h^l - C_{s,l}|| + 2$. (7) is perceived as the SPC method with the dynamic confidence degree assuring that a cluster is added if it is far from the coverage of existing clusters. (7) hints the presence of a new concept unseen in the previous observations. Hence, a data sample h^l can be regarded as a focal point. A new cluster is integrated by setting the current sample as a centroid of a new cluster $C_{(s+1),l} = h^l$ while its cardinality is set as $Car_{(s+1),l} = 1$. Note that the clustering process occurs in different levels of deep embedding space.

4.3 Parameter Learning Mechanism

Network Parameters: The parameter learning strategy of network parameters performs simultaneous feature learning and clustering in which the main goal is to establish clustering friendly latent spaces [19]. The loss function comprises two terms: reconstruction loss and clustering loss written as follows:

$$L_{all} = \underbrace{L(x, \hat{x})}_{L_1} + \sum_{l=1}^{L_{sae}} \underbrace{(L(h^l, \hat{h}^l) + \frac{\lambda}{2}||h^l - C_{win,l}||_2)}_{L_2} \tag{8}$$

where λ is a tradeoff constant controlling the influence of each loss function. (8) can be solved using the stochastic gradient descent optimizer where L_1 is executed in the end-to-end fashion while L_2 is carried out per layer, i.e., greedy layer wise fashion. $C_{win,l}$ stands for the centroid of the winning cluster of the $l - th$ layer, i.e., the closest cluster to a latent sample $win \rightarrow \min_{s=1,...,Cls_l} ||h^l - C_{s,l}||$. The first and second terms $L(x, \hat{x}), L(h^l, \hat{h}^l)$ are formed as the mean squared error (MSE) loss function where $L(x, \hat{x})$ assures data samples to be mapped back to their original representations while $L(h^l, \hat{h}^l)$ is to extract meaningful latent features in every hidden layer of SAE. The last term $||h^l - C_{win,l}||_2$ is known as the distance loss or the K-means loss producing the K-means friendly latent space. That is, a latent sample is driven to be close to the centroid of the winning hidden cluster resulting in a high cluster probability, i.e., the assignment probability of a data sample to its nearest cluster is high. The multiple nonlinear mapping via the SAE also functions as nonlinear feature reduction addressing the trivial solution as often the case of linear mapping.

Cluster Parameters: The parameter learning of hidden clusters is executed if (7) is violated meaning that a latent sample h^l is sufficiently adjacent to existing clusters. This condition only calls for association of the current latent sample to the winning cluster, the nearest cluster, fine-tuning the centroid of the winning cluster as follows:

$$C_{win,l} = C_{win,l} - \frac{(C_{win,l} - h^l)}{Car_{win,l} + 1} ; Car_{win,l} = Car_{win,l} + 1 \qquad (9)$$

The tuning process improves the coverage of the winning cluster to the current sample and thus enhances the cluster's posterior probability $\uparrow P(C_{win,l}|x)$. The intensity of the tuning process in (9) decreases as the increase of cluster's cardinality thereby expecting convergence. Only the winning cluster is adjusted here to avoid the issue of cluster's overlapping. The alternate optimization strategy is implemented in KIERA where the cluster's parameters are fixed while adjusting the network parameters and vice versa.

4.4   Centroid-Based Experience Replay

KIERA adopts the centroid-based experience replay strategy to address the catastrophic forgetting problem. This mechanism stores focal-points of previous tasks $T_1, T_2, ..., T_{k-1}$ into an episodic memory interleaved along with samples of the current task. T_t to overcome the catastrophic interference issue. Note that unlabelled images are retained in the episodic memory. The sample selection mechanism is driven by the cluster growing strategy in (7). That is, an image is considered as a focal-point x^* thus being stored in the episodic memory $M_{em}^k = M_{em}^{k-1} \cup x^*$ provided that (7) is observed. The sample selection strategy is necessary to control the size of memory as well as to substantiate the efficacy of experience replay mechanism making sure conservation of important images, focal points. Focal points represent varieties of concepts seen thus far.

The size of memory grows as the increase of tasks making the experience replay mechanism intractable for a large problem. On the other hand, the network parameters and the cluster parameters are adjusted with recent samples thereby paving possibility of the catastrophic forgetting issue. A selective sampling strategy is implemented in the centroid-based experience replay method. The goal of the selective sampling strategy is to identify the most forgotten focal points in the episodic memory for the sake of experience replay while ignoring other focal-points thereby expediting the model's updates. The most forgotten samples are those focal points which do not receive sufficient coverage of existing clusters. That is, the cluster posterior probabilities $P(C_{s,l}|x^*) = \exp{-||C_{s,l} - h_*^l||}$ of the most forgotten samples are below a midpoint mid determined:

$$mid = \frac{\sum_{n=1}^{N_{em}} \max_{s=1,...,Cls_l} P(C_{s_l}|x^*)}{N_{em}} \qquad (10)$$

where N_{em} denotes the size of episodic memory. The midpoint indicates the average level of coverage to all focal-points in the episodic memory. A focal-point is included into the replay buffer $B^* = B^* \cup x^*$ to be replayed along with the current concept if it is not sufficiently covered $P(C_{s,l}|x^*) < mid$. Finally, the centroid-based experience replay strategy is executed by interleaving images of current data batch B^k and replay buffer B^* for the training process $B^k \cup B^*$. The most forgotten focal points are evaluated by checking the current situation of network parameters and cluster parameters portrayed by the cluster posterior probability. The centroid-based experience replay strategy does not exist in our earlier work, ADCN [2].

5   Proof of Concepts

5.1   Datasets

The performance of KIERA is numerically validated using four popular continual learning problems: Permutted MNIST (PMNIST), Rotated MNIST (RMNIST), Split MNIST (SMNIST) and Split CIFAR10 (SCIFAR10). PMNIST is constructed by applying four random permutations to the original MNIST problem thus leading to four tasks $K = 4$. RMNIST applies rotations with random angles to the original MNIST problem: $[0, 30], [31, 60], [61, 90], [91, 120]$ thus creating four tasks $K = 4$ in total. The two problems characterize the concept drift problem in each task. The SMNIST presents the incremental class problem of five tasks where each task presents two mutually exclusive classes, $(0/1, 2/3, 4/5, 6/7, 8/9)$. As with the SMINST problem, the SCIFAR10 also features the incremental class problem of five tasks where each task possesses two non-overlapping target classes.

5.2   Implementation Notes of KIERA

KIERA applies an iterative training strategy for the initial training process of each task and when a new layer is added. This mechanism utilizes N_{init}^k unlabelled samples to be iterated across E number of epochs where N_{init}^k and E are respective selected as 1000 and 50 respectively. The training process completely runs in the single-pass training mode afterward. $B_0^k = \{x_i, y_i\}_{i=1}^{N_0^k}$ labelled samples are revealed for each task to associate a cluster with a target class in which for every class 100 labelled samples are offered. Hence, N_0^k is 200 for the SMNIST problem and the SCIFAR10 while N_0^k is 1000 for RMNIST and PMNIST.

5.3 Network Structure

The feature extraction layer of KIERA is realized as the convolutional neural network (CNN) where the encoder part utilizes two convolutional layers with 16 and 4 filters respectively and max-pooling layer in between. The decoder part applies transposed convolutional layers with 4 and 16 filters respectively. For PMNIST problem, the feature extraction layer is formed as a multilayer perceptron (MLP) network with two hidden layers where the number of nodes are selected as $[1000, 500]$. The random permutation of PMNIST requires a model to consider all image pixels as done in MLP. The fully connected layer is initialized as a single hidden layer $L_{sae} = 1$ with 96 hidden nodes $R_1 = 96$. The ReLU activation function is applied as the hidden nodes and the sigmoid function is implemented in the decoder output to produce normalized reconstructed images. The framework of KIERA is also applicable for complex structures.

5.4 Hyper-parameters

The hyper-parameters of KIERA are fixed across the four problems to demonstrate non ad-hoc characteristic. The learning rate, momentum coefficient and weight decay strength of the SGD method are selected as $0.01, 0.95, 5 \times 10^{-5}$ while the significant levels of the drift detector are set as $\alpha = 0.001, \alpha_d = 0.001, \alpha_w = 0.005$. The trade-off constant is chosen as $\lambda = 0.01$.

5.5 Baseline Algorithms

KIERA is compared against Deep Clustering Networks (DCN) [19], AE+KMeans and STAM [18]. DCN adopts simultaneous feature learning and clustering where the cost function is akin to KIERA (8). Nevertheless, it adopts a static network structure. AE+KMeans performs the feature learning first using the reconstruction loss while the KMeans clustering process is carried out afterward. STAM [18] relies on an irregular feature extraction layer based on the concept of patches while having a self-clustering mechanism as with KIERA. DCN and AE+KMeans are fitted with the Learning Without Forgetting (LWF) method [8] and Synaptic Intelligence (SI) method [21] to overcome the catastrophic forgetting problem. DCN and AE+KMeans make use of the same network structure as KIERA to ensure fair comparison. The regularization strength of LWF is set as $\beta = 5$ while it is allocated as 0.2 for the first task and 0.8 for the remaining task in SI method.

The hyper-parameters of STAM are selected as per their original values but hand-tuned if its performance is surprisingly poor. The baseline algorithms are executed in the same computational environments using their published codes. The performance of consolidated algorithms are examined using four evaluation metrics: prequential accuracy (Preq Acc), task accuracy (Task Acc), backward transfer (BWT) and forward transfer (FWT). Preq Acc measures the classification performance of the current task while Task Acc evaluates the classification performance of all tasks after completing the learning process. BWT and FWT are put forward in [9] where FWT indicates knowledge transfer across task, i.e., old knowledge to current task while BWT reveals knowledge retention of a model after learning a new task, i.e., new knowledge to old tasks. BWT and FWT ranges in $-\infty$ and $+\infty$ with a positive high value being the best value. All consolidated algorithms are run five times where the averages are reported in Table 1.

5.6   Numerical Results

Referring to Table 1, KIERA delivers the highest Preq accuracy and FWT in the rotated MNIST problem with statistically significant margin while being on par with STAM in the context of Task Acc. KIERA outperforms other algorithms in the PMNIST problem in which it obtains the highest Task Acc and Preq Acc with substantial differences to its competitors. Although the FWT of DCN+LWF is higher than KIERA, its Task Acc and its Preq Acc are poor. Similar finding is observed in the SCIFAR10 problem, where KIERA outperforms other algorithms in the Preq Acc, Task Acc and FWT with statistically significant differences. KIERA does not perform well only on the SMNIST problem but it is still much better than DCN and AE+KM.

Despite its competitive performance, STAM takes advantage of a non-parametric feature extraction layer making it robust against the issue of catastrophic forgetting. This module, however, hinders its execution under the GPU environments thus slowing down its execution time. The advantage of clustering-based approach is seen in the FWT aspect. Although STAM adopts the clustering approach, its network parameters are trained with the absence of clustering loss. The self-evolving network structure plays vital role here where Task Acc and Preq Acc of KIERA and STAM outperforms DCN and AE+KMeans having fixed structure in all cases with noticeable margins. The centroid-based experience replay mechanism performs well compared to SI and LWF.

Table 2 reports the network structures of KIERA and the episodic memory. The structural learning of KIERA generates a compact and bounded network structure where the number of hidden nodes, hidden layer and hidden clusters are much less than the number of data points. The hidden layer evolution is seen in the PMNIST problem where additional layers are inserted. The centroid-based experience replay excludes N_{init}^k unlabelled samples for the pre-training phase of each task. As a result, the focalpoints of the episodic memory are less than those the number of clusters.

Figure 1 exhibits the evolution of episodic memory M_{em} and replay buffer B^*. It is shown that the episodic memory M_{em} grows in much faster rate than the replay buffer B^*. Each task possesses concept changes inducing addition of new

Table 1. Numerical results of consolidated algorithms.

Datasets	Methods	BWT	FWT	Task Acc. (%)	Preq. Acc. (%)
RMNIST	KIERA	-7 ± 1.53	$\mathbf{44 \pm 1.08}$	76.84 ± 0.53	$\mathbf{79.91 \pm 0.47}$
	STAM	$\mathbf{0.9 \pm 0.35}$	$30 \pm 0.37^{\times}$	$\mathbf{77.58 \pm 0.43}$	$74.71 \pm 0.29^{\times}$
	DCN+LwF	$-15 \pm 6.54^{\times}$	$16 \pm 5.50^{\times}$	$39.47 \pm 10.13^{\times}$	$52.79 \pm 13.54^{\times}$
	DCN+SI	$-13 \pm 6.00^{\times}$	$17 \pm 6.92^{\times}$	$44.62 \pm 12.46^{\times}$	$55.66 \pm 14.83^{\times}$
	AE+KM+LwF	$-18 \pm 2.32^{\times}$	$18 \pm 1.79^{\times}$	$45.31 \pm 1.63^{\times}$	$60.15 \pm 1.54^{\times}$
	AE+KM+SI	$-9 \pm 2.72^{\times}$	$16 \pm 2.15^{\times}$	$49.07 \pm 0.73^{\times}$	$51.19 \pm 1.39^{\times}$
PMNIST	KIERA	-22 ± 3.22	2 ± 0.77	$\mathbf{59.90 \pm 2.48}$	$\mathbf{74.59 \pm 0.5}$
	STAM	$\mathbf{0.3 \pm 0.09}$	$1 \pm 0.44^{\times}$	$47.97 \pm 0.59^{\times}$	$55.37 \pm 0.26^{\times}$
	DCN+LwF	$-30 \pm 1.70^{\times}$	$\mathbf{3 \pm 1.42}$	$35.53 \pm 0.78^{\times}$	$56.50 \pm 0.54^{\times}$
	DCN+SI	$-43 \pm 3.23^{\times}$	$1 \pm 1.01^{\times}$	$33.09 \pm 2.14^{\times}$	$64.87 \pm 0.31^{\times}$
	AE+KM+LwF	$-28 \pm 1.71^{\times}$	3 ± 1.85	$35.53 \pm 1.02^{\times}$	$56.27 \pm 0.55^{\times}$
	AE+KM+SI	$-35 \pm 2.35^{\times}$	$1 \pm 1.97^{\times}$	$36.06 \pm 1.23^{\times}$	$61.50 \pm 0.36^{\times}$
SMNIST	KIERA	-9 ± 1.15	15 ± 3.56	84.29 ± 0.92	91.06 ± 0.71
	STAM	$\mathbf{-2 \pm 0.13}$	0	$\mathbf{92.18 \pm 0.32}$	$\mathbf{91.98 \pm 0.32}$
	DCN+LwF	-7 ± 3.98	18 ± 1.17	$52.42 \pm 5.02^{\times}$	$53.46 \pm 2.25^{\times}$
	DCN+SI	-4 ± 1.45	$\mathbf{22 \pm 2.89}$	$58.82 \pm 1.18^{\times}$	$57.00 \pm 0.34^{\times}$
	AE+KM+LwF	-5 ± 1.11	18 ± 1.03	$55.12 \pm 0.97^{\times}$	$54.69 \pm 0.58^{\times}$
	AE+KM+SI	-3 ± 1.88	22 ± 1.73	$58.84 \pm 0.71^{\times}$	$56.58 \pm 0.28^{\times}$
SCIFAR10	KIERA	-15 ± 5.92	$\mathbf{15 \pm 1.30}$	$\mathbf{25.64 \pm 1.85}$	$\mathbf{37.09 \pm 2.83}$
	STAM	-18 ± 2.46	$0^{\times}$	$20.60 \pm 0.66^{\times}$	35.43 ± 1.22
	DCN+LwF	-15 ± 1.32	$6 \pm 1.67^{\times}$	$14.87 \pm 1.66^{\times}$	$23.98 \pm 1.17^{\times}$
	DCN+SI	-16 ± 1.68	$6 \pm 1.90^{\times}$	$17.15 \pm 1.14^{\times}$	$25.51 \pm 0.50^{\times}$
	AE+KM+LwF	$\mathbf{-12 \pm 2.00}$	$8 \pm 0.63^{\times}$	$22.12 \pm 0.33^{\times}$	$28.77 \pm 0.84^{\times}$
	AE+KM+SI	-13 ± 1.36	$9 \pm 1.34^{\times}$	$21.91 \pm 0.68^{\times}$	$28.95 \pm 1.11^{\times}$

$^{\times}$: Indicates that the numerical results of the respected baseline and KIERA are significantly different.

Table 2. The final state of KIERA.

Datasets	NoN	NoL	NoC (K)	NoM (K)
RMNIST	101 ± 1	1 ± 0	3.2 ± 0.02	1.2 ± 0.05
PMNIST	162 ± 12	3 ± 1	5.4 ± 0.64	0.8 ± 0.15
SMNIST	95 ± 3	1 ± 0	2.8 ± 0.13	1 ± 0.1
SCIFAR10	$(1.5 \pm 2.8)K$	1 ± 0	4.2 ± 0.44	2.3 ± 0.16

NoN: total number of hidden nodes; NoL: total number of hidden layers; NoC: total number of hidden clusters; NoM: number of samples in episodic memory.

clusters and thus focal-points of the episodic memory. The selective sampling is capable of finding the most forgotten samples thus leading to bounded size of the replay buffer. The number of forgotten samples is high in the beginning of each task but reduces as the execution of centroid-based experience replay.

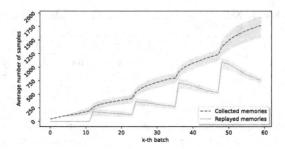

Fig. 1. The comparison of average collected and replayed memories on SMNIST problem.

6 Conclusion

This paper presents an unsupervised continual learning approach termed KIERA built upon the flexible clustering principle. KIERA features the self-organizing network structure adapting quickly to concept changes. The centroid-based experience replay is proposed to address the catastrophic forgetting problem. Our numerical study with four popular continual learning problems confirm the efficacy of KIERA in attaining high Preq Acc, high Task Acc and high FWT. KIERA delivers higher BWT than those using SI and LWF. The advantage of structural learning mechanism is also demonstrated in our numerical study where it produces significantly better performance than those static network structure. KIERA is capable of learning and predicting without the presence of Task ID and Task's boundaries. Our memory analysis deduces the effectiveness of the centroid-based experience replay in which the size of replay buffer is bounded. Our future study answers the issue of multiple streams.

References

1. Aljundi, R., Babiloni, F., Elhoseiny, M., Rohrbach, M., Tuytelaars, T.: Memory aware synapses: learning what (not) to forget. In: Ferrari, V., Hebert, M., Sminchisescu, C., Weiss, Y. (eds.) ECCV 2018. LNCS, vol. 11207, pp. 144–161. Springer, Cham (2018). https://doi.org/10.1007/978-3-030-01219-9_9
2. Ashfahani, A., Pratama, M.: Unsupervised continual learning in streaming environments. IEEE Trans. Neural Netw. Learn. Syst., 1–12 (2022). https://doi.org/10.1109/TNNLS.2022.3163362
3. Chaudhry, A., Ranzato, M., Rohrbach, M., Elhoseiny, M.: Efficient lifelong learning with A-GEM. In: 7th International Conference on Learning Representations, ICLR 2019, New Orleans, LA, USA, 6–9 May 2019. OpenReview.net (2019). https://openreview.net/forum?id=Hkf2_sC5FX
4. Gama, J.: Knowledge Discovery from Data Streams, 1st edn. Chapman & Hall/CRC (2010)
5. Hinton, G., Vinyals, O., Dean, J.: Distilling the knowledge in a neural network. arXiv preprint arXiv:1503.02531 (2015). https://arxiv.org/abs/1503.02531v1
6. Kirkpatrick, J., et al.: Overcoming catastrophic forgetting in neural networks. Proc. Natl. Acad. Sci. **114**, 3521–3526 (2017)

7. Li, X., Zhou, Y., Wu, T., Socher, R., Xiong, C.: Learn to grow: a continual structure learning framework for overcoming catastrophic forgetting. In: Proceedings of Machine Learning Research, Long Beach, California, USA, 09–15 June 2019, vol. 97, pp. 3925–3934. PMLR (2019). http://proceedings.mlr.press/v97/li19m.html

8. Li, Z., Hoiem, D.: Learning without forgetting. IEEE Trans. Pattern Anal. Mach. Intell. **40**, 2935–2947 (2018)

9. Lopez-Paz, D., Ranzato, M.: Gradient episodic memory for continual learning. In: Proceedings of the 31st International Conference on Neural Information Processing Systems, NIPS 2017, Red Hook, NY, USA, pp. 6470–6479. Curran Associates Inc. (2017)

10. Mao, F., Weng, W., Pratama, M., Yee, E.Y.K.: Continual learning via inter-task synaptic mapping. Knowl.-Based Syst. **222**, 106947 (2021). https://doi.org/10.1016/j.knosys.2021.106947. https://www.sciencedirect.com/science/article/pii/S0950705121002100

11. Paik, I., Oh, S., Kwak, T., Kim, I.: Overcoming catastrophic forgetting by neuron-level plasticity control. In: The Thirty-Fourth AAAI Conference on Artificial Intelligence, AAAI 2020, The Thirty-Second Innovative Applications of Artificial Intelligence Conference, IAAI 2020, The Tenth AAAI Symposium on Educational Advances in Artificial Intelligence, EAAI 2020, New York, NY, USA, 7–12 February 2020, pp. 5339–5346. AAAI Press (2020)

12. Parisi, G.I., Kemker, R., Part, J.L., Kanan, C., Wermter, S.: Continual lifelong learning with neural networks: a review. Neural Netw. Off. J. Int. Neural Netw. Soc. **113**, 54–71 (2019)

13. Pratama, M., Za'in, C., Ashfahani, A., Ong, Y., Ding, W.: Automatic construction of multi-layer perceptron network from streaming examples. In: Proceedings of the 28th ACM International Conference on Information and Knowledge Management (2019)

14. Rebuffi, S.A., Kolesnikov, A., Sperl, G., Lampert, C.H.: iCaRL: incremental classifier and representation learning. In: 2017 IEEE Conference on Computer Vision and Pattern Recognition (CVPR), pp. 5533–5542 (2017)

15. Rusu, A.A., et al.: Progressive neural networks. ArXiv abs/1606.04671 (2016)

16. Schwarz, J., et al.: Progress & compress: a scalable framework for continual learning. In: Dy, J., Krause, A. (eds.) Proceedings of the 35th International Conference on Machine Learning. Proceedings of Machine Learning Research, vol. 80, pp. 4528–4537. PMLR, 10–15 July 2018. https://proceedings.mlr.press/v80/schwarz18a.html

17. Shin, H., Lee, J.K., Kim, J., Kim, J.: Continual learning with deep generative replay. In: NIPS (2017)

18. Smith, J., Baer, S., Kira, Z., Dovrolis, C.: Unsupervised continual learning and self-taught associative memory hierarchies. In: 2019 International Conference on Learning Representations Workshops (2019)

19. Yang, B., Fu, X., Sidiropoulos, N.D., Hong, M.: Towards k-means-friendly spaces: simultaneous deep learning and clustering. In: Precup, D., Teh, Y.W. (eds.) Proceedings of the 34th International Conference on Machine Learning. Proceedings of Machine Learning Research, vol. 70, pp. 3861–3870. PMLR, 06–11 August 2017. http://proceedings.mlr.press/v70/yang17b.html

20. Yoon, J., Yang, E., Lee, J., Hwang, S.J.: Lifelong learning with dynamically expandable networks. In: International Conference on Learning Representations (2018)

21. Zenke, F., Poole, B., Ganguli, S.: Continual learning through synaptic intelligence. In: Proceedings of Machine Learning Research, vol. 70, pp. 3987–3995 (2017)

Evaluating Continual Learning Algorithms by Generating 3D Virtual Environments

Enrico Meloni[1,2]([✉]) [iD], Alessandro Betti[2] [iD], Lapo Faggi[1,2] [iD],
Simone Marullo[1,2] [iD], Matteo Tiezzi[1] [iD], and Stefano Melacci[1] [iD]

[1] DINFO, University of Florence, Florence, Italy
{lapo.faggi,simone.marullo}@unifi.it
[2] DIISM, University of Siena, Siena, Italy
{meloni,mtiezzi,mela}@diism.unisi.it,
alessandro.betti2@unisi.it

Abstract. Continual learning refers to the ability of humans and animals to incrementally learn over time in a given environment. Trying to simulate this learning process in machines is a challenging task, also due to the inherent difficulty in creating conditions for designing continuously evolving dynamics that are typical of the real-world. Many existing research works usually involve training and testing of virtual agents on datasets of static images or short videos, considering sequences of distinct learning tasks. However, in order to devise continual learning algorithms that operate in more realistic conditions, it is fundamental to gain access to rich, fully-customizable and controlled experimental playgrounds. Focussing on the specific case of vision, we thus propose to leverage recent advances in 3D virtual environments in order to approach the automatic generation of potentially life-long dynamic scenes with photo-realistic appearance. Scenes are composed of objects that move along variable routes with different and fully customizable timings, and randomness can also be included in their evolution. A novel element of this paper is that scenes are described in a parametric way, thus allowing the user to fully control the visual complexity of the input stream the agent perceives. These general principles are concretely implemented exploiting a recently published 3D virtual environment. The user can generate scenes without the need of having strong skills in computer graphics, since all the generation facilities are exposed through a simple high-level Python interface. We publicly share the proposed generator.

Keywords: Virtual environments · Continual learning · 3D scenario generation

1 Introduction

Traditional machine learning techniques usually assume static input data and the existence of a neat distinction between a training and a test phase. Input data,

F. Cuzzolin et al. (Eds.): CSSL 2021, LNAI 13418, pp. 62–74, 2022.
https://doi.org/10.1007/978-3-031-17587-9_5

entirely available at the beginning of the learning procedure, are processed as a whole, iterating over the training dataset multiple times, optimizing the performance with respect to a given learning task. The trained models are then freezed and exploited for inference only, hence computationally expensive re-training procedures are needed to possibly incorporate any new available information. This learning paradigm is clearly incompatible with what humans (and, more in general, animals) do in their everyday life, continuously acquiring and adapting their knowledge to the dynamic environment in which they live. The field of machine learning that aims at simulating this learning process by an artificial agent is known as continual or life-long learning [15,18]. The agent should be enough malleable to integrate new knowledge and, at the same time, enough stable to retain old information (*stability-plasticity dilemma* [1]). Vanilla neural networks have been shown to struggle in this aspect, since training a network to solve a new task will likely override the information stored in its weights (catastrophic forgetting [5,13]). In the context of computer vision (specifically, object recognition), continual learning algorithms are trained and their perfomance assessed on datasets containing static images (such as MNIST [9] or Caltech-UCSD Birds-200 [19]) or short sequences of temporally coherent frames (e.g. CORe50 [11]), usually considering a sequence of distinct learning tasks. However, the resulting learning scenarios are still far away from the original idea of an agent learning from a continuous stream of data in a real-world environment (see also the *task-free* continual learning approach of [2]). Furthermore, having the possibility to fully control the visual scene the agent perceives (number and types of objects that are present, their pose and their motion, background, possible occlusions, lighting, etc.) is essential to devise a suitable and feasible continual learning protocol and, from this point of view, real-world footages are not a viable alternative.

We thus propose to exploit the recent technological advancements in 3D virtual environments to parametrically generate photo-realistic scenes in a fully controlled setting, easily creating customizable conditions for developing and studying continual learning agents. As a matter of fact, in the last few years, due to the improved quality of the rendered scenes, 3D virtual environments have been increasingly exploited by the machine learning community for different research tasks [3,6,8,17,20,21] and different environments, based on different game engines, have been proposed so far, such as DeepMind Lab [3] (Quake III Arena engine), VR Kitchen [7], CARLA [4] (Unreal Engine 4), AI2Thor [8], CHALET [23], VirtualHome [16], ThreeDWorld [6], SAILenv [14] (Unity3D game engine), HabitatSim [17], iGibson [21], SAPIEN [22] (other engines). Moreover, the recent work [10] proposed a novel non-stationary 3D benchmark based on the VIZDoom environment to tackle model-free continual reinforcement learning.

Motivated by this significant amount of research activities, we propose to exploit such technologies to implement a method for the generation of synthetic scenes with different levels of complexity, and that depends on well-defined customizable parameters. Each scene includes dynamical elements that can be subject to random changes, making the environment a continuous source of potentially new information for continual learning algorithms. Another key aspect in the context of continual learning is related to the source of supervisions.

3D environments can naturally provide full-frame labeling for the whole stream, since the identity of the involved 3D objects is known in advance. This paves the way to the customization of active learning technologies, in which the agent asks for supervision at a certain time and coordinates, that the 3D environment can easily provide. Moreover, in the context of semi-supervised learning, it is of course straightforward to instantiate experimental conditions in which, for example, supervisions are only available during the early stages of life of the agent, while the agent is asked to adapt itself in an unsupervised manner when moving towards a new scene. On the other hand, one could also devise methods where the learning model evolves in an unsupervised manner and the interactions with the supervisor only happen at later stages of development (i.e., for evaluating the developed features). Finally, we introduce the perspective in which scenes could be just part of the same "big" 3D world, and the agent could move from one to another without abrupt interruptions of the input signal.

This paper is organized as follows. In Sect. 2, the proposed generative framework is described, where possible factors of variations will be encoded parametrically. Section 3 will present a practical implementation of these ideas extending a recent 3D virtual environment, SAILenv [14]. Some illustrative examples will be given in Sect. 4. Finally, Sect. 5 will draw some conclusions.

2 Parametric Generation of Environments

This work focusses on the problem of generating customized 3D visual environments to create experimental conditions well suited for learning machines in a *continual learning* scenario. In this section we describe the conceptual framework that allows us to formally introduce the automatic generation of a family of dynamic visual scenes. One of the main strengths of the automatic generation of 3D environments is the possibility to easily change and adapt them to facilitate the creation of benchmarks with different *degrees of difficulty* with respect to a given model and task, allowing researchers to craft ad-hoc experiments to evaluate specific skills of the continual learning model under study or to design a range of gradually harder learning problems.

The three key factors that we consider in order to devise an automatic generator of dynamic 3D scenes are visual quality, reproducibility and user-control in the generation procedure. First of all, it is important that the visual quality of the rendered scene is good enough to simulate photo-realistic conditions. On the other hand, a flexible generator should not be constrained to such high-level quality and should be able to handle also more elementary scenes in which, for instance, objects are geometric primitives or they have no or poor textures. At the same time, the generating procedure should be easy to reproduce. The dynamics of the scene should be controllable at the point in which it is possible to go back to the very beginning of the agent life to reproduce the exact same visual stream; of course, this does not exclude pseudo-randomic behaviour of the environment as, in that case, the reproducibility can be guaranteed by explicitly fixing the initial condition of the driving pseudo-random process (seed). Scenes with high visual quality and reproducible conditions can readily be obtained as soon as one relies, for the visual definition of the scenes, on a modern graphical engine which is capable of physics simulations, as we will show in our actual implementation in Sect. 3.

Concerning the capability of customizing the generated scenes, the quality of the generator depends on the flexibility it offers in terms of compositional properties and user accessibility to such properties. To this aim, we parametrically describe the visual world assuming that we have at our disposal a collection of pre-designed visual scenes $S = \{s_1, \ldots, s_n\}$. For each scene s_j, a definite collection of object templates $\Omega_j = \{\omega_{1,j}, \ldots \omega_{n_j,j}\}$ is available, where n_j is the number of object templates in the j-th scene. Each s_j is initially populated by some static instances of the object templates. The parametric generation procedure instantiates new objects from the template list, eventually including multiple instances of the same template (e.g., positioning them in different locations of the 3D space–for example, a table with *four* chairs). Formally, fixing a scene $\sigma \equiv s_j \in S$ with templates $\Omega \equiv \Omega_j$, we can define the collection of N objects that will be added to σ by the parametric generation procedure as $\Phi := (\varphi_1, \ldots, \varphi_N) \in \Omega^N$. For example, given a scene with templates $\Omega = \{\texttt{chair}, \texttt{pillow}, \texttt{laptop}\}$, we could have $\Phi = (\texttt{chair1}, \texttt{chair2}, \texttt{pillow1}, \texttt{laptop1})$, where $N = 4$ and we used numerical suffixes to differentiate repeated instances of the same object template.

In this work, we assume that the lighting conditions of the rendering engine are fixed and so the position and the orientation of the agent point of view.[1] We denote with $(v_k)_{k \in \mathbb{N}}$ the sequence of frames captured by the agent point of view. Hence, σ can be generated once Φ is chosen and the following attributes are specified for each φ_i:

- the indices $(k_i, \hat{k}_i) \in \mathbb{N}^2$ of the frames where φ_i makes respectively its first and last appearance;
- the position and the orientation of the object in the frame k_i, collectively represented as a vector[2] $\pi_i \in \mathbb{R}^6$;
- its trajectory (i.e., its position and orientation) for each k such that $k_i < k \leq \hat{k}_i$, modeled by a set of parameters indicated with τ_i and defined in what follows.

Notice that, in order to grant additional flexibility to the scenario definition, it is useful to allow the possibility of dynamically spawning new objects on the fly, when the agent is already living in the generated environment. This property enables the creation of scenes that might also significantly change over time, being expanded or connected to other scenes, capabilities that might be very appropriate in the context of continual learning. The values of $(k_i, \hat{k}_i)$, π_i, and τ_i, for $i = 1, \ldots, N$ are regarded as parameters that characterize

---

[1] Here we are making this assumption in order to simplify the management of the generation procedure, however these settings can be regarded as additional parameters that can be chosen to define the environment.

[2] Again, for the sake of simplicity, we are assuming to work with objects which are rigid bodies (hence the $\mathbb{R}^6$) but indeed this is by no means a crucial assumption.

the customizable objects visible in a frame k. In particular, parameters τ_i, $i = 1, \ldots, N$ unambiguously define the object trajectories, such as the trajectory's global shape, the speed and whether or not the trajectory completely lies in the agent's field of view. Formally, considering the i-th object, we have that $\tau_i = (\kappa_i, \vartheta_i^1, \ldots, \vartheta_i^m)$, where κ_i specifies the chosen kind of trajectory while $\vartheta_i^1, \ldots, \vartheta_i^m$ stand for all the additional parameters required to fully determine it. Overall, the visual environment is specified by the collection of parameters $\Theta := (k_1, \ldots, k_N, \hat{k}_1, \ldots, \hat{k}_N, \pi_1, \ldots, \pi_N, \tau_1, \ldots, \tau_N)$.

Hence it is clear that through the choice of Θ we can control the number of objects present at any given frame k, the position and orientations of the objects, the way in which objects moves and their velocity, i.e., the nature of their trajectories and whether or not objects escape the field of view. A fine control over this set of parameters provide us with a general tool to create highly customizable datasets suitable for continual learning scenarios, possibly of increasing difficulty with respect to a given learning task. For example, in an object recognition problem, the number of angles from which an object is seen, which is closely related to the chosen trajectory, could clearly affect the visual complexity of the task.

Fig. 1. The three default scenes of SAILenv, `room01`, `room02`, `room03` (besides the empty scene `object_view`).

3   Continual Learning 3D Virtual Benchmark

SAILenv [14] is a platform specifically designed to ease the creation of customizable 3D environments and their interface with user-defined procedures. With a few lines of code, any learning algorithm can get several data from the virtual world, such as pixel-level annotations. SAILenv includes a Unity library with ready-to-go 3D objects and it provides basic tools to allow the customization of a virtual world within the Unity 3D editor, without the need of writing 3D graphics specific code. Differently from the other existing solutions, it also offers motion information for each pixel of the rendered view. SAILenv is based on the Unity Engine[3], a state-of-the-art graphics and physics engine that is commonly used for videogames and physical simulations. It therefore presents

---

[3] See https://unity.com.

realistic objects and scenes, with fine details and realistic illumination, while allowing the creation of credible motion dynamics of objects in the scene. The SAILenv platform, when executed, creates the virtual world, managing the physical simulation in all its aspects. It also opens up a network connection listener, which waits for incoming connections to interact with the environment. The communication is implemented with low-level socket operations and a custom protocol which focuses on achieving high performance, avoiding bottlenecks in data exchange that would excessively slow down every simulation, for reasons not-related to machine learning.

The platform is released with a Python API, which offers a high-level interface, called *Agent*, that acts as the main player in the communication between the 3D world and custom Python code. The API allows the creation of multiple agents that "live" in the virtual world, each of them with its own view of the environment. Each agent is defined by several parameters, such as the resolution of the rendered image that is acquired from the 3D scene, its position and orientation. By means of a few lines of code, an agent can return fully-annotated views of the environment:

```python
from sailenv.agent import Agent

agent = Agent(width=256, height=192,
              host="192.168.1.3", port=8085)
agent.register()
agent.change_scene(agent.scenes[2])

while True:
    frame_views = agent.get_frame()
    ...

agent.delete()
```

The data (`frame_views`) provided by the agent include: the *RGB View* (pixel colors of the rendered scene), *Optical Flow* (motion)[4], *Semantic Segmentation* (category-level labels), *Instance Segmentation* (instance-level labels), and *Depth View* (depth). Each of these elements contains pixel-wise dense annotations. They are all generated in real-time, and they are then transmitted to the Python client with a fast low-level communication mechanism. This facilitates the use of the SAILenv platform in real-time online learning scenarios.

For the purpose of this work, we extended the SAILenv platform to support dynamic scene generation following the guidelines of Sect. 2. The new Python API we developed also allows the customization of the scene without having to deal with 3D-graphics editing tools or the Unity Editor, creating new objects on-demand.

---

[4] A pixel of the Optical Flow View is a vector $(v_x, v_y) \in \mathbb{R}^2$ representing the velocity in px/frame. For visualization purposes (e.g. see the Optical Flow rows of Figs. 5, 6, 7), each vector could be converted in polar coordinates (ρ, ϕ) and the pixel could be assigned the HSV color $(\phi, 1, \rho)$. Therefore, ρ would determine the intensity of the color (the faster, the brighter), while ϕ would determine the color (red: left, green: down, cyan: right, violet: up).

Scenes and Objects. We extended the SAILenv Python API to allow an easy and quick definition of the parameters in Θ, through few lines of code. After having registered the Agent in the environment (as shown in the previous code snippet), a pre-designed scene σ can be chosen using the method `agent.change_`⌋ `scene(scene_name)`. In particular, SAILenv comes with the following scenes, $S =$ {`object_view` (empty space), `room01` (bedroom), `room02` (living room), `room03` (bathroom)} (see Fig. 1). Selecting a scene automatically determines the set Ω of available templates. Given a certain template, a new object φ_i can be generated through the method `agent.spawn_object(template_name, position, rotation[,` `dynamic, limited_to_view])`, specifying its position, rotation and, in the case of a moving object, the properties of the associated trajectory (last two arguments). This method will return an `object_id`. Invoking the creation at frame k will spawn the selected object at the next frame ($k_i = k + 1$) and it will set π_i to the concatenation of the given position and rotation. We postpone the description of the trajectory dynamics (`dynamic` argument) to the next paragraph, while when the Boolean flag `limited_to_view` is set to true, the object will be always kept withing the field of view of the agent. The condition for making this choice effective is to create invisible barriers where the object will bounce, located at the borders of the agent camera frustum (that is the region of 3D world seen by the agent), by calling `agent.spawn_collidable_view_frustum()`. The object can then be deleted through the method `agent.despawn_object(object_id)` which is equivalent to setting $\hat{k}_i$ to the identifier of the next frame.

Trajectories. The object dynamics can be defined through simple Python classes. In this work, we propose three different types of trajectories, associated to classes that can be instantiated by calling: `LinearWaypoints(waypoints_list,` `total_time)`, `CatmullWaypoints(waypoints_list, total_time)`, `UniformMovement` `RandomBounce(speed, angular_speed, start_direction[, seed])`. Within the notation of Sect. 2, the chosen class trajectory for the i-th object is what we formalized with κ_i (for example, consider κ_i set to `UniformMovementRandomBounce`), while the associated arguments (`speed, angular_speed, start_direction`⌋ `[, seed]`, in the case of the previous example) stand for $\vartheta_i^1, \ldots, \vartheta_i^4$. Both `CatmullWaypoints` and `LinearWaypoints` require a list of L waypoints $(w_1, \ldots, w_L) \in (\mathbb{R}^6)^L$ and the time (in seconds) that the object takes to loop around all of them, see Fig. 2 for an example of code (described in the next section). The difference between the two dynamics is that the former does a linear interpolation between two consecutive waypoints, while the latter computes a Catmull-Rom Spline interpolation [12] along the whole set of waypoints. Collisions with other scene elements are handled by the Unity physics engine, that takes care of rejoining the trajectory whenever it becomes possible. `UniformMovementRandomBounce` makes an object move inertially until it hits another one or the edges of the agent view. After the collision, the object bounces back in a random direction and also acquires an additional random torque. The `speed` and the `angular_speed` parameters limit the velocity of the object in the scene, the `start_direction` bootstraps its movement and the `seed` may be fixed to replicate the same dynamics (i.e., for reproducibility purposes). Furthermore, the API allows to change the object position and orientation at any given time through the method `agent.move_object(object_id, position, rotation)`.

Utilities. What we described so far fully defines the scene and the parameters in Θ. In order to simplify the management of the Python code, we added a higher abstraction level based on the Python class `Scenario` and some additional utility classes, such as `Waypoint` and `Object`, that allow to describe the structure of the scene in a compact manner, as we will show in the examples of Sect. 4 (Figs. 2, 3 and 4). When using class Scenario, the object trajectories can be orchestrated through the `Timings` classes. There are three different available timings. The first one, `AllTogether(wait_time)`, makes every object move at the same time after `wait_time` seconds. The second, `WaitUntilComplete`, supports only waypoint-based dynamics (more, generally, dynamics that are based on loops), and activates them one at a time waiting until each one is complete before starting the next one. Finally, the `DictTimings(_map)` timing takes as input a map that defines for each trajectory how long it should be active before stopping and starting the next one. Finally, we mention the `Frustum` class to simplify the creation of the previously described invisible boundaries, if needed.

4   Examples

The proposed SAILenv-based generator can be downloaded at SAILenv official website https://sailab.diism.unisi.it/sailenv/. In the following we show three examples of generations.

```
scene = "object_view/scene"
waypoints = [
    Waypoint(Vector3(0., 0., 4.), Vector3(0., 0., 0.)),
    ...
    Waypoint(Vector3(-5., 1., 7.), Vector3(90., 90., 180.))
]
dynamic = CatmullWaypoints(waypoints=waypoints, total_time=10.0)
objects = [
    Object("c1", "Cylinder",
            Vector3(0, 0, 2), Vector3(0, 0, 0), dynamic)
]
scenario = Scenario(scene, objects)
agent.load_scenario(scenario)
```

Fig. 2. A Cylinder moves through the defined waypoints, with a trajectory obtained by Catmull interpolation.

```
scene = "room_02/scene"
dynamic1 = UniformMovementRandomBounce(seed=32,
                    speed=0.8, start_direction=Vector3(0, 5, 2))
dynamic2 = UniformMovementRandomBounce(...)
dynamic3 = UniformMovementRandomBounce(...)
agent_pos = agent.get_position()
objects = [
    Object("c1", "Chair 01",  agent_pos + Vector3(2, 0, 0),
           Vector3(0, 0, 0),  dynamic1, frustum_limited=True),
    Object("p1", "Pillow 01", ...),
    Object("d1", "Dish 01", ...)
]
timings = AllTogetherTimings(0.75)
view_limits = Frustum(True, 10.)
scenario = Scenario(scene, objects, timings, view_limits)
agent.load_scenario(scenario)
```

Fig. 3. Definition of a simple scenario where a Chair, a Pillow and a Dish move pseudo-randomly around a pre-built living room.

Example 1. In Fig. 2 the SAILenv basic scene named `object_view` is chosen, that is an empty space with monochrome background. Then, a set of way-points is defined and the dynamic `CatmullWaypoints` is created using them. A single object is specified, named `c1`, based on template `Cylinder`, at position `Vector3(0,0,2)` and with an initial orientation specified by `Vector3(0,0,0)` (Euler angles); here `Vector3(_,_,_)` is the description of a three dimensional vector. The `CatmullWaypoints` dynamics will move the Cylinder through each way-point, interpolating the trajectory with a Catmull-Rom spline. Using the notation presented in Sect. 2, we have: $\sigma = $ `object_view`, $\Omega = \{\ldots, \text{Cylinder}, \ldots\}$, $\Phi = (\text{c1})$, $(k_1, \hat{k}_1) = (0, \infty)$ and the associated trajectory is specified by $\kappa_1 = $ `CatmullWaypoints`, $\vartheta_1^1 = $ `waypoints` and $\vartheta_1^2 = $ `total_time` $= 10$. The generated RGB view and the corresponding optical flow are shown in Fig. 5 considering four different time instants.

```
scene = "room_01/scene"
waypoints = [
    Waypoint(Vector3(0.5, 1.4, 0.5), Vector3(0., 0., 0.)),
    Waypoint(Vector3(0.3, 1., -1.), Vector3(90., 0., 0.)),
    ...
]
agent_pos = Vector3(-1.3, 2., 1.5)
agent.set_position(agent_pos)
agent.set_rotation(Vector3(22., 144., 0))
dynamic = CatmullWaypoints(waypoints=waypoints)
objects = [
    Object("racket", "Tennis Racket 01",
           Vector3(0.5, 1.4, 0.5), Vector3(0., 0., 0.), dynamic)
]
scenario = Scenario(scene, objects)
agent.load_scenario(scenario)
```

Fig. 4. A Tennis Racket moves along a set of waypoints (Catmull interpolation) inside a pre-built bedroom.

Example 2. In Fig. 3 the selected pre-designed scene is room_02, a realistic living room with common furniture. The novel SAILenv API allows us to add new objects that, in this case, are a chair, a pillow and a dish, from the templates Chair 01, Pillow 01 and Dish 01. They are initially located in specific points relative to the agent's position (agent_pos + Vector3(_,_,_)) with a certain orientation (the second Vector3(_,_,_)). For all the objects, the dynamic UniformMovementRandomBounce is chosen, also specifying their speed, their initial direction and the seed to ensure the reproducibility of the pseudorandom bounces. Finally, the AllTogetherTimings configuration is selected, making every object move at the same time within the view frustum of the agent and also never going beyond 10 m of distance from the agent itself (view_₁ limits=Frustum(**True**, 10.)). Using the notation of Sect. 2, we have σ = room_02, Ω = {...,Chair 01, ...,Pillow 01, ..., Dish 01,...}, Φ = (c1, p1, d1) and $(k_i, \hat{k}_i) = (0, +\infty) \; \forall \; i$. Moreover, κ_i = UniformMovementRandomBounce with possible different ϑ_i^m (seed, speed, start_direction) $\forall \; i$. For an illustration of the final result, see Fig. 6 (RGB view, semantic segmentation and optical flow).

Example 3. Finally, the code in Fig. 4 illustrates another realistic scene (bedroom) in which a tennis racket moves according to the CatmullWaypoints dynamic. The selected waypoints are defined at the beginning of the script, toghether with the initial position and orientation of the racket. According to the notation of Sect. 2, we have σ = room_01, Φ = (racket) from the template Tennis Racket 01 and $(k_i, \hat{k}_i) = (0, +\infty) \; \forall i$. In this last case, κ_i = CatmullWaypoints and ϑ_1^1 = waypoints. The final result is shown in Fig. 7. Notice that we also used SAILenv facilities to change the position and orientation of the agent.

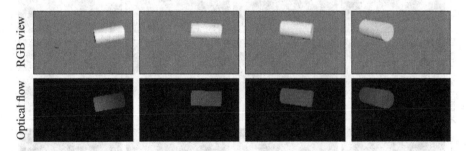

Fig. 5. Scene described by the script in Fig. 2. Four frames are shown (from left to right)—RGB view and optical flow.

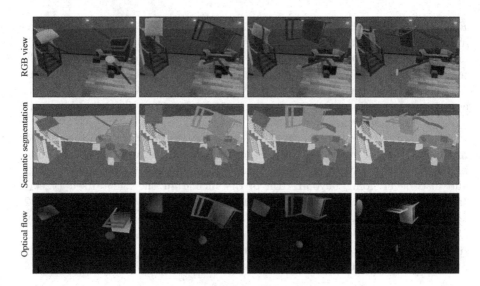

Fig. 6. Scene described by the script in Fig. 3 (room02—livingroom scene) considering four different frames (from left to right). For each object, the chosen dynamic is UniformMovementRandomBounce. For each frame we display the RGB view, the semantic segmentation and the optical flow. Additionally, we depict in the RGB and semantic segmentation views the local trajectories followed by the moving objects (attached to the moving objects).

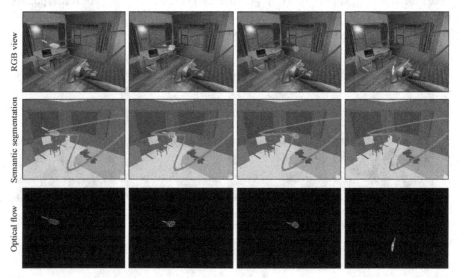

Fig. 7. Scene described by the script in Fig. 4 (room01—bedroom scene) considering four different frames (from left to right). The chosen dynamic is CatmullWaypoints. For each frame we display the RGB view, the semantic segmentation and the optical flow. Additionally, we depict in the RGB and semantic segmentation views the full trajectory followed by the moving object (attached to the racket).

5   Conclusions

In this paper we have proposed the idea of generating fully customizable datasets to train and test continual learning agents through the use of 3D-virtual environments. Describing the generating process of the scenes parametrically allows the user to have full control on the final visual stream the agent perceives and, given a certain learning task, to create scenarios of increasing difficulty. We have reported a concrete realization of these ideas in the SAILenv virtual environment, showing the potential effectiveness of this approach.

Acknowledgements. This work was partially supported by the PRIN 2017 project RexLearn (Reliable and Explainable Adversarial Machine Learning), funded by the Italian Ministry of Education, University and Research (grant no. 2017TWNMH2).

References

1. Abraham, W.C., Robins, A.: Memory retention-the synaptic stability versus plasticity dilemma. Trends Neurosci. **28**(2), 73–78 (2005)
2. Aljundi, R., Kelchtermans, K., Tuytelaars, T.: Task-free continual learning. In: Proceedings of the IEEE/CVF Conference on Computer Vision and Pattern Recognition, pp. 11254–11263 (2019)
3. Beattie, C., Leibo, J.Z., Teplyashin, D., Ward, T., Wainwright, M., Küttler, H., et al.: Deepmind lab. arXiv:1612.03801 (2016)
4. Dosovitskiy, A., Ros, G., Codevilla, F., Lopez, A., Koltun, V.: CARLA: an open urban driving simulator. In: Conference on Robot Learning, pp. 1–16. PMLR (2017)
5. French, R.M.: Catastrophic forgetting in connectionist networks. Trends Cogn. Sci. **3**(4), 128–135 (1999)
6. Gan, C., Schwartz, J., Alter, S., Schrimpf, M., et al.: Threedworld: a platform for interactive multi-modal physical simulation. arXiv:2007.04954 (2020)
7. Gao, X., Gong, R., Shu, T., Xie, X., Wang, S., Zhu, S.C.: VRKitchen: an interactive 3D virtual environment for task-oriented learning. arXiv:1903.05757 (2019)
8. Kolve, E., et al.: AI2-THOR: an interactive 3D environment for visual AI. arXiv:1712.05474 (2017)
9. Lecun, Y., Bottou, L., Bengio, Y., Haffner, P.: Gradient-based learning applied to document recognition. Proc. IEEE **86**(11), 2278–2324 (1998). https://doi.org/10.1109/5.726791
10. Lomonaco, V., Desai, K., Culurciello, E., Maltoni, D.: Continual reinforcement learning in 3D non-stationary environments. In: Proceedings of the IEEE/CVF Conference on Computer Vision and Pattern Recognition Workshops, pp. 248–249 (2020)
11. Lomonaco, V., Maltoni, D.: CORe50: a new dataset and benchmark for continuous object recognition. In: Conference on Robot Learning, pp. 17–26. PMLR (2017)
12. Maggini, M., Melacci, S., Sarti, L.: Representation of facial features by Catmull-Rom splines. In: Kropatsch, W.G., Kampel, M., Hanbury, A. (eds.) CAIP 2007. LNCS, vol. 4673, pp. 408–415. Springer, Heidelberg (2007). https://doi.org/10.1007/978-3-540-74272-2_51

13. McCloskey, M., Cohen, N.J.: Catastrophic interference in connectionist networks: the sequential learning problem. In: Psychology of Learning and Motivation, vol. 24, pp. 109–165. Elsevier (1989)
14. Meloni, E., Pasqualini, L., Tiezzi, M., Gori, M., Melacci, S.: SAILenv: learning in virtual visual environments made simple. In: 25th International Conference on Pattern Recognition, ICPR 2020, pp. 8906–8913 (2020)
15. Parisi, G.I., Kemker, R., Part, J.L., Kanan, C., Wermter, S.: Continual lifelong learning with neural networks: a review. Neural Netw. **113**, 54–71 (2019)
16. Puig, X., et al.: VirtualHome: simulating household activities via programs. In: Proceedings of the IEEE Conference on Computer Vision and Pattern Recognition, pp. 8494–8502 (2018)
17. Savva, M., Kadian, A., Maksymets, O., et al.: Habitat: a platform for embodied AI research. In: Proceedings of the IEEE/CVF International Conference on Computer Vision, pp. 9339–9347 (2019)
18. Van de Ven, G.M., Tolias, A.S.: Three scenarios for continual learning. arXiv preprint arXiv:1904.07734 (2019)
19. Wah, C., Branson, S., Welinder, P., Perona, P., Belongie, S.: The Caltech-UCSD Birds-200-2011 Dataset. Technical report, CNS-TR-2011-001, California Institute of Technology (2011)
20. Weihs, L., et al.: Allenact: a framework for embodied AI research. arXiv:2008.12760 (2020)
21. Xia, F., et al.: Interactive gibson benchmark: a benchmark for interactive navigation in cluttered environments. IEEE Robot. Autom. Lett. **5**(2), 713–720 (2020)
22. Xiang, F., Qin, Y., Mo, K., et al.: SAPIEN: a simulated part-based interactive environment. In: Proceedings of the IEEE/CVF Conference on Computer Vision and Pattern Recognition, pp. 11097–11107 (2020)
23. Yan, C., Misra, D., Bennnett, A., Walsman, A., Bisk, Y., Artzi, Y.: Chalet: cornell house agent learning environment. arXiv:1801.07357 (2018)

A Benchmark and Empirical Analysis for Replay Strategies in Continual Learning

Qihan Yang[1] , Fan Feng[2] , and Rosa H. M. Chan[2](✉)

[1] Imperial College London, London SW7 2AZ, UK
[2] City University of Hong Kong, Tat Chee Avenue, Kowloon, Hong Kong, China
rosachan@cityu.edu.hk

Abstract. With the capacity of continual learning, humans can continuously acquire knowledge throughout their lifespan. However, computational systems are not, in general, capable of learning tasks sequentially. This long-standing challenge for deep neural networks (DNNs) is called *catastrophic forgetting*. Multiple solutions have been proposed to overcome this limitation. This paper makes an in-depth evaluation of the **memory replay methods**, exploring the efficiency, performance, and scalability of various sampling strategies when selecting replay data. All experiments are conducted on multiple datasets under various domains. Finally, a practical solution for selecting replay methods for various data distributions is provided.

Keywords: Continual learning · Memory replay

1 Introduction

Unlike human beings who have continual learning ability, deep neural networks (DNNs), in general, suffer from a significant function decline or forgets the previously learned knowledge when encountering novel information and tasks. Extensive approaches have been proposed to overcome this limitation, including the regularization method (e.g., learning without Forgetting (LwF) [18], elastic weight consolidation (EWC) [12]), dynamic architecture method (e.g., Progressive neural networks (PNN) [23]), and the memory replay method (e.g., deep generative replay (DGR) [26]). The regularization method regularizes the gradient descent path and tries to minimize the loss for new tasks while restricting the change of specific parameters to maintain the memory for the previous tasks. The dynamic architecture approach allocates new neural resources when the model is facing novel tasks. The memory replay method, proven to have the best performance [14], rehearses the learned data from either a data buffer (i.e., experience replay) or a generative model (i.e., generative replay) and jointly trains the neural network with both old task and novel task data.

Several benchmarks are proposed to evaluate the continual learning in computer vision tasks, including general computer vision [19,27], and robotic vision

F. Cuzzolin et al. (Eds.): CSSL 2021, LNAI 13418, pp. 75–90, 2022.
https://doi.org/10.1007/978-3-031-17587-9_6

tasks [25]. However, these benchmarks only focus on specific datasets. Meanwhile, a wide range of continual learning methods is compared in these works, which are not equipped with the in-depth analysis of memory-based methods. In our work, we only focus on the analysis of replay-based methods, which are the most effective and practical methods, using different datasets. To provide this comprehensive benchmark, we evaluate various memory-based replay strategies (including random, confidence, entropy, margin, K-means, core-set, maximally interfered retrieval (MIR), and Bayesian dis-agreement), replaying complex and simple data, and the difference between experience replay and generative replay. Using the standard continual learning datasets (i.e., MNIST [16], CIFAR-10 [15], MiniImagenet [6], and OpenLORIS-Object [25]), we conduct 46 experiments in total.

2   Memory Replay

Among all continual learning approaches, memorization-based approaches using experience replay have generally proven more successful than their regularization-based alternatives [14]. There are, in general, two typical ways to get the replay data: *experience replay* and *generative replay*.

2.1   Experience Replay

Early attempts of continual learning use the experience replay approach [22] (Fig. 1), which introduces a memory buffer that stores previous task data and regularly replay old samples interleaved with new task data. Specifically, when a new task comes with input data x and labels y, the model will also load a subsample (bx, by) from the buffer (N_s represents the number of subsamples), and then a replay data $(\mathrm{mem\_}x, \mathrm{mem\_}y)$ is chosen from the subsamples based on *certain criteria* (N_r represents the number of replay data and N_c represents the number of classes). The model performs training on both the current-task and the replay data. After training, the current task data will be stored in the buffer. As a result, the model can acquire the novel knowledge and maintain some previous memory simultaneously.

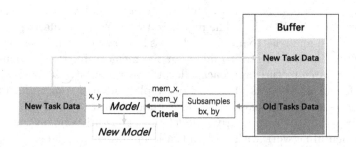

Fig. 1. The workflow of experience replay.

2.2 Generative Replay

When the training data for old tasks are not available, only pseudo-inputs and pseudo-targets produced by a memory network can be fed into the model [22]. This rehearsal technique, named generative replay (Fig. 2), does not require extra memory storage but introduces a generative model parallel with the classifier, such as variational auto-encoder (VAE) [11], Generative adversarial network (GAN) [8], and Wasserstein GAN (WGAN) [2]. At any training stage, the generative model can produce pseudo data $\tilde{x}$, which imitates the old data that have been trained; the classifier can correctly classify the tasks that have been traversed and give pseudo prediction $\tilde{y}$ based on $\tilde{x}$. When the new task comes with input data x and labels y, both the generative model and the classifier are jointly trained with $(\tilde{x}, \tilde{y})$ and (x, y). After training, the generative model will be capable of producing pseudo data that mimic both the previous tasks and the current task data; the classifier will be able to classify both the old tasks and novel task correctly.

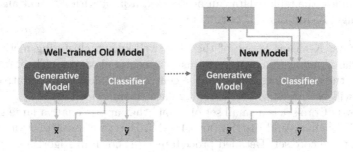

Fig. 2. The workflow of generative replay.

3   Evaluation

This paper evaluates 8 replay strategies, which can be classified as random selection, feature embedding, model prediction, and maximal interference.

- *Model Prediction*: entropy, confidence, margin, Bayesian dis-agreement, and MIR;
- *Feature Embedding*: K-means and core-set.
- *Random sampling*.

With the random replay (randomly choosing N_r replay data from N_s sub-samples) as a benchmark, we explored the open problems with multiple datasets under various domains.

1. the efficiency, performance, and scalability of different sampling strategies when selecting replay data;
2. the relationship between the efficiency and the difficulty of replay data;

3. the performance gap between experience replay and generative replay methods;
4. the relationship between the performances and continual learning orders.

Based on the empirical findings and analysis, we also provide a practical solution for selecting replay methods for datasets under different domains.

3.1 Feature Embedding

We use ResNet-18 [9] in the experience replay methods. For simplicity, the output features of layer1, layer2, and layer3 are modified to 20, 40, and 80. The current classifier takes the subsamples $bx = [bx^1, \dots, bx^{N_s}]$ as input, and the output of layer3 will be extracted as feature maps. Notice the dimension of these maps is $(N_s, 80, \star, \star)$. Then, a 2D adaptive average pooling layer will extract the feature vector with dimension $(N_s, 80, 1, 1)$ from the feature maps, followed by a flatten layer stretches the feature vectors to the embeddings $e = [e^1, \dots, e^{N_s}]$ with each e^i for $i \in \{1, \dots, N_s\}$ has a dimension of $(N_s, 80)$. After getting the embeddings for subsamples, the replay data can be selected from it with different algorithms (embeddings' **K-means** and **core-set**).

- **K-means**: K-means is one of the most well-known clustering method [20]. With the N_s embeddings, it performs a N_r center clustering. Then, from each cluster, the embedding closest to the centre is the most representative point, which will be chosen to be the replay data (mem_x, mem_y).
- **Core-set**: Core-set is a small set of points that approximate a large group of the point's shape and distribution [4,5,24]. Here, we use *Max-Min Distance* to select the core-set. Detailed procedures are shown in Algorithm 1.

Algorithm 1: Max-Min Distance Algorithm

Result: Get N_r representative replay data from N_s subsamples
Input: Randomly select an embedding e^i as the initial point, $i \in \{1, \dots, N_s\}$; mark the initial point as *"selected"* point; mark all the other embeddings as *"unselected"* points.
repeat
- For all the *unselected* points, cluster them to the *selected* points based on the minimal distance;
- Select the embedding with the maximum minimal distance as the subsequent replay data;
- Mark the new embedding as the *selected* point.

until N_r *embeddings have been marked as "selected"*;

3.2   Model Prediction

Besides strategies based on feature embedding, there are four popular strategies based on the model prediction. The current model takes the subsamples as input, performs an evaluation, and gets the predictions with size (N_s, N_c). For any subsample bx^i for $i \in \{1, \ldots, N_s\}$, the prediction is given $\hat{by}^i = [\hat{by}_1^i, \ldots, \hat{by}_{N_c}^i]$. With this prediction, the replay data (mem_x, mem_y) can be selected based on different calculation methods (**confidence, entropy, margin**, and **Bayesian dis-agreement**).

– **Confidence (C)**: For any subsample bx^i for $i \in \{1, \ldots, N_s\}$, the *Confidence* C^i is given by its largest class prediction $\hat{by}_{max}^i$ among all the $\hat{by}_c^i$ for $c \in \{1, \ldots, N_c\}$ (Eq. 1). A large confidence stands for simple replay data and a small confidence stands for difficult replay data.

$$C^i \left(\hat{by}^i \mid bx^i \right) = \hat{by}_{max}^i = \max \left(\hat{by}_1^i, \ldots, \hat{by}_{N_c}^i \right) \tag{1}$$

  • Simple replay: top N_r largest C^i, $i \in \{1, \ldots, N_s\}$.
  • Difficult replay: top N_r smallest C^i, $i \in \{1, \ldots, N_s\}$.

– **Entropy (H)**: Entropy denotes the *randomness* or the *uncertainty* of the data. From the model prediction $\hat{by}^i = [\hat{by}_1^i, \ldots, \hat{by}_{N_c}^i]$, the *Entropy* H^i can be calculated with Eq. 2 for any subsample bx^i for $i \in \{1, \ldots, N_s\}$. Similarly, a small entropy stands for high certainty (simple) replay data and a large entropy stands for low certainty (difficult) replay data [28].

$$H^i \left(\hat{by}^i \mid bx^i \right) = -\sum_{c=1}^{N_c} \left(\hat{by}_c^i \times \log \hat{by}_c^i \right) \tag{2}$$

  • Simple replay: top N_r smallest H^i, $i \in \{1, \ldots, N_s\}$.
  • Difficult replay: top N_r largest H^i, $i \in \{1, \ldots, N_s\}$.

– **Margin (M)**: For any subsample bx^i for $i \in \{1, \ldots, N_s\}$, with its prediction $\hat{by}^i = [\hat{by}_1^i, \ldots, \hat{by}_{N_c}^i]$, the *Margin* M^i is given by difference between the largest class prediction $\hat{by}_{max}^i$ and the smallest class prediction $\hat{by}_{min}^i$ (Eq. 3). A large margin stands for simple replay data, and a small margin stands for difficult replay data [3].

$$M^i \left(\hat{by}^i \mid bx^i \right) = \hat{by}_{max}^i - \hat{by}_{min}^i$$

$$= \max \left(\hat{by}_1^i, \ldots, \hat{by}_{N_c}^i \right) - \min \left(\hat{by}_1^i, \ldots, \hat{by}_{N_c}^i \right) \tag{3}$$

  • Simple replay: top N_r largest M^i, $i \in \{1, \ldots, N_s\}$.
  • Difficult replay: top N_r smallest M^i, $i \in \{1, \ldots, N_s\}$.

- **Bayesian Dis-agreement (B)**: Bayesian dis-agreement strategy is inherited from the *(Bayesian Active Learning by Dis-agreement* (BALD) [7]. This method takes the assumption that there are some model parameters control the dependence between inputs and outputs. As a result, an acquisition function is defined to estimate the mutual information between the model parameters and the model predictions. In other words, it captures how strongly the model parameters and the model predictions for a given data point are coupled [10].

  Given a model $\mathcal{M}$ with parameter ω, a training set $\mathcal{D}_{\text{train}}$, the Bayesian dis-agreement B^i for a subsample bx^i for $i \in \{1, \ldots, N_s\}$ is calculated with Eq. 4.

$$B^i \left(\hat{by}^i, \omega \mid bx^i, \mathcal{D}_{\text{train}} \right) = H \left(\hat{by}^i \mid bx^i, \mathcal{D}_{\text{train}} \right) - \mathbb{E}_{p(\omega \mid \mathcal{D}_{\text{train}})} [H(\hat{by}^i \mid bx^i, \omega)] \tag{4}$$

The first term $H \left(\hat{by}^i \mid bx^i, \mathcal{D}_{\text{train}} \right)$ is the *Entropy* of the model prediction. For given dataset, the first term is small if the model prediction is certain. The second term $\mathbb{E}_{p(\omega \mid \mathcal{D}_{\text{train}})} [H(\hat{by}^i \mid bx^i, \omega)$ is an expectation of the entropy of the model prediction over the posterior of the model parameters. For each draw of model parameters from the posterior, the second term is small if the model prediction is certain [13].

In general, the input will have a large B if its model prediction is prone to vary with changing model parameters and vice versa. A small Bayesian dis-agreement represents stable (simple) replay data, and a large bayesian dis-agreement represents unstable (difficult) replay data.

- Simple replay: top N_r smallest B^i, $i \in \{1, \ldots, N_s\}$.
- Difficult replay: top N_r largest B^i, $i \in \{1, \ldots, N_s\}$.

For any subsample, it will get k predictions based on distinct parameters with the help of a drop out layer; then the first term of the acquisition function can be calculated as the entropy of the mean of the k predictions, and the second term can be calculated as the mean of the k entropy (Fig. 3).

3.3   Maximal Interfered Retrieval (MIR)

The crucial idea of MIR is to filter out the samples which will be maximally interfered by the new task data [1]. The interference is measured by the difference between the loss value before and after training the novel data. To get the loss after training the new task data, MIR performs a *virtual update* according to the gradients generated during training the novel data.

The loss function of the classifier is represented by Eq. 5, and the virtual update can be seen as Eq. 6.

$$\mathcal{L} \left(\mathcal{M}_\omega \left(x \right), y \right) \tag{5}$$

$$\omega^v = \omega - \eta \nabla \mathcal{L} \left(\mathcal{M}_\omega \left(x \right), y \right) \tag{6}$$

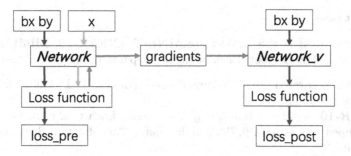

Fig. 3. The workflow of MIR: the green arrows denote the forward propagation of new data x; the red arrows denote the back propagation of new data; the blue arrows denote the prediction procedure of subsamples. (Color figure online)

For any subsample bx^i for $i \in \{1, \ldots, N_s\}$, with its prediction $\hat{by}^i$, current model $\mathcal{M}_\omega$ and virtual updated model $\mathcal{M}_{\omega^v}$, the MIR score S^i is calculated with Eq. 7.

$$S^i = \mathcal{L}^v - \mathcal{L}$$
$$= \mathcal{L}\left(\mathcal{M}_{\omega^v}\left(bx^i\right), by^i\right) - \mathcal{L}\left(\mathcal{M}_\omega\left(bx^i\right), by^i\right) \tag{7}$$

A lower score means that the subsample is less affected by the new data; a higher score represents that the subsample is more affected by the new data, and those high score data will be selected as replay data. The detailed algorithm is shown in Algorithm 2.

Algorithm 2: Maximal Interfered Retrieval algorithm

Result: Get N_r most interfered replay data from N_s subsamples.
Input: new task data (x, y), subsamples (bx, by);
Given: Model $\mathcal{M}$ parameters ω;
- Train the model $\mathcal{M}_\omega$ with new data (x, y) and record the gradients $\nabla \mathcal{L}$;
- Copy the current model to a new model, perform virtual update based on the gradients, and get the virtual model $\mathcal{M}_{\omega^v}$;
- Evaluate the subsamples (bx, by) with both the current model and the virtual model, get two losses $\mathcal{L}, \mathcal{L}^v$;
- Calculate the MIR score $S = \mathcal{L}^v - \mathcal{L}$;
- Select replay data: (mem_x, mem_y) is the (bx, by) with the top N_r largest S^i, for $i \in \{1, \ldots, N_s\}$.

3.4   Datasets

The datasets used in this project are **MNIST, CIFAR-10, MiniImagenet,** and **OpenLORIS-Object**. Each of them is separated into several tasks.

- **MNIST**: separated into 5 disjointed tasks. For each task, $1,000$ samples are used for training.
- **CIFAR-10**: separated into 5 disjointed tasks. Each task consists of 2 non-overlapped classes with $9,750$ training data, 250 validation data, and $2,000$ test data.
- **MiniImagenet**: divided into 20 disjointed tasks with 5 categories each. Each task consists of 2400 training images.
- **OpenLORIS-Object**: separated into four tasks based on the four factors, and each task has all 121 classes.

4   Results and Discussion

4.1   Evaluation Criteria

Three evaluation criteria are used to denote the model performance. Assume a given dataset $\mathcal{D}$ has T tasks $\mathcal{T}_1, \ldots, \mathcal{T}_T$. After training the last task $\mathcal{T}^T$, the *Accuracy* and *Forgetting rate* is given by Eq. 8 and Eq. 9. The $Acc_{\mathcal{T}_i}$ represents the accuracy for task $\mathcal{T}_i$ after training the last task, and the $Best_{\mathcal{T}_i}$ represents the best accuracy for task $\mathcal{T}_i$ during the whole training procedure. Usually the $Best_{\mathcal{T}_i}$ is achieved right after the $\mathcal{T}_i$ just be trained.

$$\text{Accuracy} = \frac{1}{T} \sum_{i=1}^{T} Acc_{\mathcal{T}_i} \tag{8}$$

$$\text{Forgetting Rate} = \frac{1}{T} \sum_{i=1}^{T} (Best_{\mathcal{T}_i} - Acc_{\mathcal{T}_i}) \tag{9}$$

The third criteria *Average Time* is the average running time for a single run. Given total running time T_r and number of runs n_r, the average time (s) is calculated by Eq. 10.

$$\text{Average Time} = \frac{T_r}{n_r} \tag{10}$$

4.2   Replay Strategies Comparison

When comparing different replay strategies, all other factors are set to default: experience replay with simple data. Eight replay strategies are trained with the same settings under same conditions, and compared parallel. The detailed results are shown in Table 1. The **highest accuracy**, the **lowest forgetting rate**, and the **minimal running time** (besides random replay) are embolden. The recordings of the *maximal running time* are italic. Table 2 and 3 summarize the results.

Table 1. Replay strategies comparison result.

		Random	Least entropy	Largest confidence	Largest margin	Least Bayesian dis-agreement	K-means	Core-set	MIR
MNIST	Accuracy	0.870 ± 0.012	0.871 ± 0.014	0.869 ± 0.009	**0.876 ± 0.014**	**0.876 ± 0.010**	**0.876 ± 0.008**	0.870 ± 0.010	0.871 ± 0.014
	Forgetting rate	0.105 ± 0.015	0.101 ± 0.019	0.099 ± 0.014	0.099 ± 0.017	0.099 ± 0.014	**0.096 ± 0.010**	0.100 ± 0.013	0.101 ± 0.018
	Average time (s)	3.050	3.900	**3.700**	3.850	5.150	*22.400*	4.150	4.350
CIFAR-10	Accuracy	0.339 ± 0.024	0.393 ± 0.020	0.402 ± 0.018	0.400 ± 0.018	0.395 ± 0.009	0.349 ± 0.018	0.345 ± 0.018	**0.409 ± 0.013**
	Forgetting rate	0.400 ± 0.040	0.267 ± 0.036	0.259 ± 0.036	0.274 ± 0.035	**0.221 ± 0.018**	0.373 ± 0.031	0.351 ± 0.026	0.248 ± 0.019
	Average time (s)	62.400	**89.200**	90.067	89.800	234.333	*282.933*	89.267	152.133
MiniImagenet	Accuracy	0.107 ± 0.010	0.116 ± 0.016	0.134 ± 0.018	0.134 ± 0.022	**0.158 ± 0.014**	0.111 ± 0.012	0.109 ± 0.018	0.126 ± 0.015
	Forgetting rate	0.402 ± 0.012	0.364 ± 0.013	0.348 ± 0.026	0.334 ± 0.027	**0.280 ± 0.020**	0.382 ± 0.013	0.358 ± 0.022	0.338 ± 0.037
	Average time (s)	1183.000	1290.800	**1284.400**	1284.400	1622.800	*1745.800*	1465.500	1379.600
OpenLORIS	Accuracy	0.960 ± 0.000	**0.966 ± 0.004**	**0.966 ± 0.007**	0.964 ± 0.011	0.962 ± 0.004	0.962 ± 0.004	0.962 ± 0.004	0.964 ± 0.007
	Forgetting rate	0.022 ± 0.007	**0.014 ± 0.004**	0.020 ± 0.010	0.018 ± 0.010	0.024 ± 0.004	0.016 ± 0.007	0.026 ± 0.009	0.020 ± 0.010
	Average time (s)	5521.800	**5777.000**	9582.000	12017.400	*12270.400*	7400.600	8828.200	6753.600

Table 2. Highest accuracy, lowest forgetting rate, least average time, and largest average time achieved on each dataset.

	Accuracy	Forgetting rate	Least average time (s)	Largest average time (s)
MNIST	0.876	0.096	3.700	22.400
CIFAR-10	0.409	0.221	89.200	282.933
MiniImagenet	0.158	0.280	1284.400	1745.800
OpenLORIS	0.966	0.014	5777.000	12270.400

Table 3. Best performances of different replay strategies on the CIFAR-10, MiniImagenet and OpenLORIS-Object.

	Accuracy	Forgetting rate	Least average time (s)	Largest average time (s)
CIFAR-10	MIR	Bayesian	Entropy	K-means
MiniImagenet	Bayesian	Bayesian	C. & M.	K-means
OpenLORIS	H. & C.	Entropy	Entropy	Bayesian

For MNIST, almost all the replay strategies achieve a similar result, and the performances are, by and large, reasonably good (accuracy **0.870**, forgetting rate **0.100**). The reason behind this might be that MNIST is too simple, and no matter choose what kind of replay data, even using random selected data, makes no significant difference. However, for a slightly diverse dataset like CIFAR-10, the general accuracy is lower, and the forgetting rate is higher (accuracy between **0.339** to **0.409** and a forgetting rate between **0.221** to **0.400**). For more complex dataset like MiniImagenet, the accuracy drop exponentially, and the forgetting problem is more severe (accuracy between **0.107** to **0.158** and a forgetting rate between **0.280** to **0.402**). OpenLORIS-Object also has complex data distribution, but it achieves an accuracy between **0.960** to **0.966** and a forgetting rate between **0.014** to **0.022**. Nevertheless, this outstanding performance is not comparable to the other datasets due to the task separation difference.

In the continual learning field, there are different *Incremental Learning Scenarios* as follow:

- **Instance incremental**: The class number is fixed, while in each learning stage, more novel instances are involved.
- **Class-incremental**: New classes are introduced in each learning stage.
- **Domain-incremental**: The class number is also fixed; however, the model will be used in the context of a different but related input distribution.

The tasks for MNIST, CIFAR-10, and MiniImagenet are in a class-incremental manner. Each time the classifier will encounter new categories that it has not seen before. However, for OpenLORIS-Object, with all classes being presented in the first task, the following tasks are trying to perform similar classification to the same categories under different environmental factors. This follows the domain-incremental manner. The difficulty for training a class-incremental model is much greater than training a domain-incremental model. Thus, the forgetting rate for OpenLORIS-Object is generally lower than that in the other three datasets.

For CIFAR-10 and MiniImagenet and OpenLORIS-Object, different replay strategies show their uniqueness.

- **Bayesian Dis-agreement**: Bayesian dis-agreement has an outstanding performance on the CIFAR-10 and MiniImagenet; however, its forgetting rate on the OpenLORIS-Object increases dramatically compared with other strategies. The class number could be a problem. CIFAR-10 only has **2** classes per task (5 tasks and 10 categories in total), and MiniImagenet has **5** classes per task (20 tasks and 100 categories in total). However, OpenLORIS-Object includes all the **121** classes for each task. This outcome implies that the Bayesian dis-agreement strategy has good performance with a small class number, but it has **low scalability**.

   Intuitively, when the class number gets larger, the mutual information between the model parameters and output prediction will be more complex and ambiguous; thus, the Bayesian dis-agreement strategy will fail to select the representative replay data based on that mutual information.
- **Entropy, confidence, and margin**: These three methods have neutral performances for any dataset. Since they select the replay data only based on the model prediction, the results are more stable and **plastic**: They neither have a satisfying result as Bayesian dis-agreement on CIFAR-10 and MiniImagenet nor suffer performance decay when the class number gets more extensive as in OpenLORIS-Object. Moreover, the training time for these three methods, in general, are less than Bayesian dis-agreement, K-means, and MIR. As a result, for complex datasets with large data scale and class number, these three methods might be the most efficient choices.

- **MIR**: Theoretically, MIR should be the best method since it tries to replay the data that interfered the most with the new coming data. Practically, it does not show its overwhelming advantage.

  On the one hand, the subsample size N_s may not be sufficient for MIR to traverse enough learned data and determine the most interfered samples. On the other hand, the prior assumption for MIR - replay the data with the largest loss difference between before and after training the new data will reinforce the old memory - is reasonably correct, but may not be as efficient as studying the model output directly as entropy, confidence, and margin strategies. It also takes time to evaluate the interference by making the prediction twice with both the current model and virtual updated model. Consequently, MIR strategy producing limited improvement, consumes more time than the model prediction-based strategies.
- **K-means and core-Set**: K-means method is very time consuming, and it has a slight improvement when the data is simple and the class number is low. Similarly, a small class number and the limited number of subsamples may not be sufficient for K-means to provide meaningful clusters and discover valuable replay data. core-Set strategy is also optimal considering its running time and the optimization effect it has.

4.3 Replay Data Difficulty Comparison

Entropy, confidence, margin, and Bayesian dis-agreement can be used to compare the difference between replay simple data and replay difficult data. Detailed results are shown in Table 4. The **better performance** in accuracy (higher), forgetting rate (lower), and average time (shorter) are embolden. For MNIST, replay simple data and replay difficult data does not have clear distinctions. However, for CIFAR-10 and MiniImagenet, replaying difficult data generally lead to higher accuracy and lower forgetting rate. The running time for the two cases are comparable.

Table 4. Replay data difficulty comparison results.

		Replay simple data				Replay difficult data			
		Least entropy	Largest confidence	Largest margin	Least Bayesian disagreement	Largest entropy	Least confidence	Largest margin	Largest Bayesian disagreement
MNIST	Accuracy	0.871 ± 0.014	0.869 ± 0.009	$\mathbf{0.876 \pm 0.014}$	$\mathbf{0.876 \pm 0.010}$	$\mathbf{0.877 \pm 0.008}$	$\mathbf{0.874 \pm 0.009}$	0.872 ± 0.014	0.876 ± 0.009
	Forgetting rate	0.101 ± 0.019	0.099 ± 0.014	$\mathbf{0.099 \pm 0.017}$	$\mathbf{0.099 \pm 0.014}$	$\mathbf{0.095 \pm 0.010}$	$\mathbf{0.098 \pm 0.016}$	0.100 ± 0.019	0.101 ± 0.014
	Average time (s)	3.900	$\mathbf{3.700}$	$\mathbf{3.850}$	5.150	$\mathbf{3.700}$	4.000	4.100	4.750
CIFAR-10	Accuracy	0.393 ± 0.020	0.402 ± 0.018	0.400 ± 0.018	0.395 ± 0.009	$\mathbf{0.402 \pm 0.017}$	$\mathbf{0.403 \pm 0.011}$	$\mathbf{0.407 \pm 0.013}$	$\mathbf{0.403 \pm 0.008}$
	Forgetting rate	0.267 ± 0.036	0.259 ± 0.036	0.274 ± 0.035	0.221 ± 0.018	$\mathbf{0.244 \pm 0.028}$	$\mathbf{0.233 \pm 0.023}$	$\mathbf{0.247 \pm 0.017}$	$\mathbf{0.211 \pm 0.018}$
	Average time (s)	89.200	90.067	89.800	234.333	89.933	91.667	$\mathbf{88.733}$	235.800
MiniImagenet	Accuracy	0.116 ± 0.016	0.134 ± 0.018	0.134 ± 0.022	$\mathbf{0.158 \pm 0.014}$	$\mathbf{0.122 \pm 0.007}$	$\mathbf{0.146 \pm 0.018}$	$\mathbf{0.136 \pm 0.029}$	0.148 ± 0.017
	Forgetting rate	0.364 ± 0.013	0.348 ± 0.026	$\mathbf{0.334 \pm 0.027}$	0.280 ± 0.020	$\mathbf{0.358 \pm 0.004}$	$\mathbf{0.322 \pm 0.031}$	0.336 ± 0.025	$\mathbf{0.260 \pm 0.032}$
	Average time (s)	1290.800	1284.400	1284.400	1622.800	$\mathbf{1266.000}$	$\mathbf{1267.000}$	$\mathbf{1280.400}$	1607.200

4.4 Experience and Generative Replay Comparison

MNIST is used to compare the efficiency of experience replay and generative replay. The generative replay uses VAE model [11]. The results for experience replay and generative replay comparison are shown in the Table 5. The replay data samples during training each task and the reconstruction images for 5 tasks are shown in Fig. 4 and 5.

Table 5. MNIST ER and GR comparison results.

MNIST		Experience replay	Generative replay
Evaluation criteria	Accuracy	**0.870 ± 0.012**	0.563 ± 0.005
	Forgetting rate	**0.105 ± 0.015**	0.486 ± 0.007
	Average time (s)	**3.050**	6.754

According to the result, the experience replay has higher accuracy, lower forgetting rate, and less time than the generative replay. On the one hand, the generated data do not faithfully imitate the original image due to the replay model's imperfections. On the other hand, training the generative model introduces extra time consumption. Following the conclusion in [17], the generative replay has worse performance on complex dataset such as CIFAR-10, and continual learning with generative replay remains a challenge.

4.5 Training Sequence Comparison

Since the OpenLORIS-Object dataset splits the data difficulty into three levels, the difference between training the hard data (weak illumination, high occlusion rate, small object size or longer distance from the camera, complex environment) first, and training the easy data (strong illumination, low occlusion rate, big object size or short distance from the camera, simple environment) first could be explored and evaluated. The result is shown in Table 6. According to the result, learn the data with small environmental interfered (low difficulty level) and simple data distribution first, then moving to the challenging training samples (high difficulty level) helps the model get higher final accuracy and lower forgetting rate.

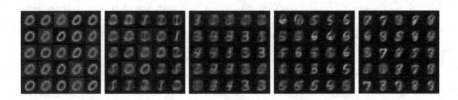

Fig. 4. The replay data samples for each task.

Fig. 5. The reconstruction image samples for the five tasks.

Table 6. OpenLORIS-Object training sequence comparison results.

OpenLORIS		Easy first	Hard first
Evaluation criteria	Accuracy	**0.096 ± 0.000**	0.095 ± 0.016
	Forgetting rate	**0.022 ± 0.007**	0.034 ± 0.020
	Average time (s)	5521.800	**5294.400**

4.6 Analysis

Based on the experimental results[1], we draw the concluding remarks:

- With the same setting, experience replay can achieve better accuracy and a lower forgetting rate compared with generative replay, but it needs an extra working memory to store all previous data. This may lead to memory problem when the task number gets larger or the scale of the dataset is large.
- Under experience replay, for a simple dataset like MNIST, different replay strategies make no significant difference, and they all achieve reasonable good accuracy and a low forgetting rate. For slightly complex datasets like CIFAR-10 or even more challenging dataset like MiniImagenet, Bayesian dis-agreement leads to a good forgetting rate when the categories per task are small. However, Bayesian dis-agreement has low scalability, and it is relatively time-consuming.
- MIR improves the performance compared to random replay, but it also takes more time to train than model prediction-based methods. Moreover, it is not guaranteed to get the lowest forgetting rate or the best accuracy. Embedding based methods like K-means and core-set are not ideal under the same training condition compared with other methods. Thus, for a complex dataset with a large class number for any single take, simple replay strategies like entropy, confidence, and margin are the most effective approaches.

---

[1] All the methods are implemented using PyTorch [21] toolbox with an Intel Core i9 CPU and 4 Nvidia RTX 2080 Ti GPUs.

– Replay difficult data is, in general, more optimal for the continual learning model to achieve a low forgetting rate. For OpenLORIS-Object, train the model with objects under simple environmental factors first slightly improves the model performance.

5 Conclusion

This paper provides a benchmark and empirical analysis on the replay-based methods, which are theoretically proven to be the best-performing methods in continual learning [14]. The extensive experiments with various sampling strategies are conducted under different datasets. Based on our analysis, the continual learning problem certainly needs further research, since for complex datasets, even with advanced replay strategies, the accuracy remains low, and the forgetting rate remains high. This work would shed some light on selecting replay methods for various data distributions and lay a solid foundation for further theoretical studies.

References

1. Aljundi, R., et al.: Online continual learning with maximal interfered retrieval. In: Wallach, H., Larochelle, H., Beygelzimer, A., d'Alché-Buc, F., Fox, E., Garnett, R. (eds.) Advances in Neural Information Processing Systems, vol. 32. Curran Associates, Inc. (2019). https://proceedings.neurips.cc/paper/2019/file/15825aee15eb335cc13f9b559f166ee8-Paper.pdf

2. Arjovsky, M., Chintala, S., Bottou, L.: Wasserstein generative adversarial networks. In: Precup, D., Teh, Y.W. (eds.) Proceedings of the 34th International Conference on Machine Learning. Proceedings of Machine Learning Research, vol. 70, pp. 214–223. PMLR (2017). http://proceedings.mlr.press/v70/arjovsky17a.html

3. Balcan, M.-F., Broder, A., Zhang, T.: Margin based active learning. In: Bshouty, N.H., Gentile, C. (eds.) COLT 2007. LNCS (LNAI), vol. 4539, pp. 35–50. Springer, Heidelberg (2007). https://doi.org/10.1007/978-3-540-72927-3_5

4. Borsos, Z., Mutny, M., Krause, A.: Coresets via bilevel optimization for continual learning and streaming. In: Larochelle, H., Ranzato, M., Hadsell, R., Balcan, M.F., Lin, H. (eds.) Advances in Neural Information Processing Systems, vol. 33, pp. 14879–14890. Curran Associates, Inc. (2020). https://proceedings.neurips.cc/paper/2020/file/aa2a77371374094fe9e0bc1de3f94ed9-Paper.pdf

5. Campbell, T., Beronov, B.: Sparse variational inference: Bayesian coresets from scratch (2019)

6. Deng, J., Dong, W., Socher, R., Li, L.J., Li, K., Fei-Fei, L.: Imagenet: a large-scale hierarchical image database. In: 2009 IEEE Conference on Computer Vision and Pattern Recognition, pp. 248–255. IEEE (2009)

7. Gal, Y., Islam, R., Ghahramani, Z.: Deep Bayesian active learning with image data. In: Precup, D., Teh, Y.W. (eds.) Proceedings of the 34th International Conference on Machine Learning. Proceedings of Machine Learning Research, vol. 70, pp. 1183–1192. PMLR, International Convention Centre, Sydney, Australia (2017). http://proceedings.mlr.press/v70/gal17a.html

8. Goodfellow, I.J., et al.: Generative adversarial nets. In: Proceedings of the 27th International Conference on Neural Information Processing Systems, NIPS 2014, vol. 2, pp. 2672–2680. MIT Press, Cambridge (2014)

9. He, K., Zhang, X., Ren, S., Sun, J.: Deep residual learning for image recognition. In: Proceedings of the IEEE Conference on Computer Vision and Pattern Recognition (CVPR) (2016)

10. Houlsby, N., Huszár, F., Ghahramani, Z., Lengyel, M.: Bayesian Active Learning for Classification and Preference Learning. arXiv e-prints arXiv:1112.5745 (2011)

11. Kingma, D.P., Welling, M.: Auto-encoding variational bayes. arXiv preprint arXiv:1312.6114 (2013)

12. Kirkpatrick, J., et al.: Overcoming catastrophic forgetting in neural networks. Proc. Natl. Acad. Sci. **114**(13), 3521–3526 (2017). https://doi.org/10.1073/pnas.1611835114. https://www.pnas.org/content/114/13/3521

13. Kirsch, A., Amersfoort, J., Gal, Y.: Batchbald: efficient and diverse batch acquisition for deep bayesian active learning (2019, submitted)

14. Knoblauch, J., Husain, H., Diethe, T.: Optimal continual learning has perfect memory and is NP-hard. In: III, H.D., Singh, A. (eds.) Proceedings of the 37th International Conference on Machine Learning. Proceedings of Machine Learning Research, vol. 119, pp. 5327–5337. PMLR (2020). http://proceedings.mlr.press/v119/knoblauch20a.html

15. Krizhevsky, A., Nair, V., Hinton, G.: CIFAR-10 (Canadian institute for advanced research). http://www.cs.toronto.edu/~kriz/cifar.html

16. LeCun, Y., Cortes, C.: MNIST handwritten digit database (2010). http://yann.lecun.com/exdb/mnist/

17. Lesort, T., Caselles-Dupré, H., Garcia-Ortiz, M., Stoian, A., Filliat, D.: Generative models from the perspective of continual learning. In: 2019 International Joint Conference on Neural Networks (IJCNN), pp. 1–8 (2019). https://doi.org/10.1109/IJCNN.2019.8851986

18. Li, Z., Hoiem, D.: Learning without forgetting. IEEE Trans. Pattern Anal. Mach. Intell. **40**(12), 2935–2947 (2018). https://doi.org/10.1109/TPAMI.2017.2773081

19. Lomonaco, V., Maltoni, D.: Core50: a new dataset and benchmark for continuous object recognition. In: Conference on Robot Learning, pp. 17–26. PMLR (2017)

20. MacQueen, J., et al.: Some methods for classification and analysis of multivariate observations. In: Proceedings of the Fifth Berkeley Symposium on Mathematical Statistics and Probability, Oakland, CA, USA, pp. 281–297 (1967)

21. Paszke, A., et al.: Pytorch: an imperative style, high-performance deep learning library. In: Neural Information Processing Systems (NeurIPS), pp. 8024–8035 (2019)

22. Robins, A.: Catastrophic forgetting, rehearsal and pseudorehearsal. Connect. Sci. **7**(2), 123–146 (1995). https://doi.org/10.1080/09540099550039318

23. Rusu, A.A., et al.: Progressive neural networks. arXiv abs/1606.04671 (2016)

24. Sener, O., Savarese, S.: Active learning for convolutional neural networks: a core-set approach. In: International Conference on Learning Representations (2018). https://openreview.net/forum?id=H1aIuk-RW

25. She, Q., et al.: Openloris-object: a robotic vision dataset and benchmark for lifelong deep learning. In: 2020 IEEE International Conference on Robotics and Automation (ICRA), pp. 4767–4773 (2020). https://doi.org/10.1109/ICRA40945.2020.9196887

26. Shin, H., Lee, J.K., Kim, J., Kim, J.: Continual learning with deep generative replay. In: Guyon, I., et al. (eds.) Advances in Neural Information Processing Systems, vol. 30. Curran Associates, Inc. (2017). https://proceedings.neurips.cc/paper/2017/file/0efbe98067c6c73dba1250d2beaa81f9-Paper.pdf

27. Van de Ven, G.M., Tolias, A.S.: Three scenarios for continual learning. arXiv preprint arXiv:1904.07734 (2019)

28. Wang, D., Shang, Y.: A new active labeling method for deep learning. In: 2014 International Joint Conference on Neural Networks (IJCNN), pp. 112–119 (2014). https://doi.org/10.1109/IJCNN.2014.6889457

SPeCiaL: Self-supervised Pretraining for Continual Learning

Lucas Caccia[1,2(✉)] and Joelle Pineau[1,2]

[1] MILA, McGill University, Montreal, Canada
`lucas.page-caccia@mail.mcgill.ca`
[2] Facebook AI Research, Montreal, Canada

Abstract. This paper presents SPeCiaL: a method for unsupervised pretraining of representations tailored for continual learning. Our approach devises a meta-learning objective that differentiates through a sequential learning process. Specifically, we train a linear model over the representations to match different augmented views of the same image together, each view presented sequentially. The linear model is then evaluated on both its ability to classify images it just saw, and also on images from previous iterations. This gives rise to representations that favor quick knowledge retention with minimal forgetting. We evaluate SPeCiaL in the Continual Few-Shot Learning setting, and show that it can match or outperform other supervised pretraining approaches.

Keywords: Continual learning · Unsupervised learning · Meta learning

1 Introduction

In Machine Learning, practitioners often rely on the ubiquitous assumption that the training data is sampled independently and identically from a fixed distribution. This iid assumption is a convenient requirement, spanning from classical approaches to Deep Learning based methods. Yet, the world that humans encounter is far from static: the data we observe is temporally correlated, and changes constantly. Therefore many practical applications, from autonomous driving to conversational chatbots, can greatly benefit from the ability to learn from non-stationary data.

To this end, the field of Continual Learning [17,23] tackles the problem setting where an agent faces an online and non-stationary data stream. The core of CL methods have been intently focused on directly minimizing catastrophic interference, a phenomenon whereby previously acquired knowledge gets overwritten as the agent learns new skills.

In this paper, we are interested in the deployment of CL systems [10]. Namely, we are interested in *preparing* a system before its deployment on non-stationary data where it will need to make predictions and accumulate knowledge in an online fashion. We believe this setting captures better the deployment of CL systems in real life, as it would be more realistic to deploy an agent with some - albeit limited - knowledge of the world.

F. Cuzzolin et al. (Eds.): CSSL 2021, LNAI 13418, pp. 91–103, 2022.
https://doi.org/10.1007/978-3-031-17587-9_7

Therefore, we ask ourselves how can we equip agents with data representations that are amenable to learning under non-stationarity? An innovative solution was first proposed by [21], coined *Online-Aware Meta Learning* (OML). This objective differentiates through a supervised sequential learning task and optimizes for minimal forgetting. While ingenious, OML requires access to labelled data, which can be difficult or expensive to obtain for many CL scenarios. For example, is it fairly cheap to obtain large unlabelled datasets from a dashboard camera in the hopes of training a self-driving agent. However, manually annotating each frame - or even deciding which types of annotation - can be time consuming and costly.

In this work, we instead aim to learn representations amenable to CL purely from unlabelled data. Recently, the field of unsupervised representation learning (or self-supervised learning) has shown tremendous progress [14], closing the gap with fully supervised methods on large-scale image datasets. Moreover, SSL methods have shown better transfer capabilities [14] to out-of-distribution data than supervised methods. To this end, we leverage key components of recent SSL methods, enabling us to devise an efficient label-free representation learning algorithm for CL. Concretely, our contributions are as follows:

- We propose a novel strategy, called SPeCiaL, for unsupervised pretraining of representations amenable to continual learning
- Our algorithm efficiently reuses past computations, reducing its computational and memory footprint.
- We show that SPeCiaL can match or outperform OML on several continual few-shot learning benchmarks.

2   Related Work

Our work builds upon several research fields, which we summarize here.

Self-supervised Learning. The field of Unsupervised Learning of Visual Representations has made significant progress over the last few years, reducing the gap with supervised pretraining on many downstream tasks. By using data augmentations, SSL methods can generate pseudo-labels, matching different augmented views of the same image together. Instance-level classifiers [14,15] treat each image - and its augmented versions - as its own class, and rely on noise contrastive estimation to compare latent representations. Clustering Methods [11] instead group latent instances together, either using the cluster id as a label, or ensuring cluster consistency across different views of the same image. In general, SSL methods are not designed to be deployed in non-stationary settings, which can lead to suboptimal performance (see Sect. 5). Our proposed method addresses this specific issue.

Continual Learning. The supervised CL literature is often divided into several families of methods, all with the principal objective of reducing catastrophic forgetting. In the fixed architecture setting we have *prior based methods* [23,27,38],

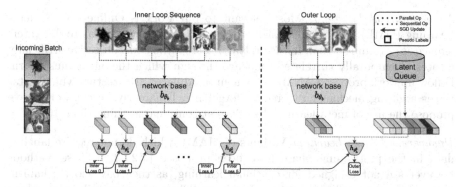

Fig. 1. Workflow of our proposed method, SPeCiaL. From the incoming batch we create a temporally correlated sequence with augmentations from the same image shown next to each other. Augmentations of the same image are assigned a unique label, which the model learns during the inner loop. In the outer loop the model is evaluated both on its retention of the seen sequence, but also on past samples seen in previous updates. The encoder base b_θ extracts all representations in parallel, leaving only the linear head h_ϕ to run sequentially. (Color figure online)

which regularize the model to limit the change of parameters deemed important in previous tasks. *Rehearsal based methods* [2,13], fight forgetting by replaying past samples alongside the incoming data. This data can be store in a small episodic memory [3] or sampled from a generative model also trained continually [32,35]. Some replay based methods further aim at directly optimizing for the reduction of negative interference across tasks [12,18,26,31].

Unsupervised Continual Learning. Several works [1,29,33] learn representations in an unsupervised manner over non-iid data. We also note that some generative replay methods also fit into this category, namely ones where the generator does not leverage labelled data [9,32]. This line of work differs from the setting explored in this paper, as the representation learning occurs not during pretraining (where we assume iid acess to some data) but over a stream of non-stationary data.

Meta-Learning. The Meta-Learning [30,34,36] - or learning to learn - field aims to design models which can acquire new skills or knowledge fast, via a small set of examples. Most of the literature has focused on the few-shot supervised learning setting, where agents are first pretrained offline and evaluated on their ability to label new classes given small support sets. Model-Agnostic Meta-Learning (MAML) [16] enables agents to learn a parameter initialization suitable for fast adaption, by directly optimizing through the update procedure performed by the model at deployment time. The flexibility of MAML has led its use to reach beyond few-shot learning.

Meta-continual Learning. Most relevant to our work is Online-Aware Meta-Learning (OML) [21], which designs a meta-objective using catastrophic interference as a training signal. In the pretraining step, the OML objective artificially creates a temporally correlated sequence through which the agent must learn. Follow up work proposed ANML [7], a neuromodulated architecture which meta-learns a gating mechanism to reduce forgetting. Differently, recent works have propose the use of meta-learing objectives at continual-learning time [10,18].

Unsupervised Meta-Learning Variants of MAML which do not require labelled data in the pretraining phase have been proposed [5,20,22]. These methods however are not designed for continual learning, as they have no mechanism to prevent catastrophic forgetting. Lastly and closest to our work is [8], where the authors propose a unsupervised pretraining strategy for learning representations in the continual few shot learning setting. Similar to [20], the authors use an unsupervised embedding function with clustering to label examples, which are then used within the OML algorithm, resulting in a 3-step procedure for the pretraining phase. Our work instead proposes a simplified (single step) pretraining procedure, which is both conceptually simpler, and is easier to extend.

3   Background: Meta Continual Learning

In this section we formalize the learning setting under which our proposed method operates. We begin by first defining the general continual learning setting, in which (potentially pretrained) agents are deployed. We then describe meta-continual learning, a framework to pretrain agents before deployment in a continual learning setting.

We follow [21,26] and define a Continual Learning Problem (CLP) as a potentially infinite stream of samples:

$$\mathcal{S} = (X_1, Y_1), (X_2, Y_2), \ldots, (X_t, Y_t), \ldots,$$

where input X_t and output Y_t belong to sets $\mathcal{X}$ and $\mathcal{Y}$ respectively. Crucially, examples are not drawn i.i.d from a fixed distribution over (X, Y) pairs. Instead, we assume that at each timestep t, input samples are drawn according to the conditional distribution $P(X_t|C_t)$, where $C_t \in \mathcal{C}$ is a hidden *time-dependent context variable* [10], denoting the state of the distribution at time t. In practice, C_t can be the previous frames of a video, or the cards currently dealt in a poker game. Given this context variable, samples can be drawn i.i.d. from $P(X_t|C_t)$, in other words the C_t encapsulates all the non-stationarity of the CLP.

Our goal is to learn a θ-parameterized predictor $f_\theta : \mathcal{X} \to \mathcal{Y}$ which can be queried *at any given time* on samples belonging to previously seen contexts $C_{\leq t}$. For simplicity, we assume that the target function is determinisic and only depends on the input, i.e. $p(Y|X,C) = p(Y|X)$. Our goal is to minimize the following objective after T timesteps

$$\mathcal{L}_{CLP}(\theta) \stackrel{\text{def}}{=} \mathbb{E}\big[\ell(f_\theta(X), Y)\big] = \sum_{t=1}^{T} \mathbb{E}_{p(x|C_t)}\big[\ell(f_\theta(X), Y)\big] \qquad (1)$$

where $\ell : \mathcal{Y} \times \mathcal{Y} \to \mathbb{R}$ denotes a loss function between the model predictions and labels.

Meta CL. In Meta Continual Learning, the goal is to pretrain the predictor f_θ for better performance, or transfer, on the CLP objective. In the *pretraining* phase, we aim to learn parameters θ, such that at *deployment* time, the model can quickly adapt to any given CLP. To do so, we adopt the nested optimization procedure described in MAML [16] for the pretraining step. In the inner loop, we sample a sequence of contexts $C_1, ..., C_k$ from a distribution over context sequences $p(\mathcal{C}^k)$. From this sequence, we then generate a trajectory $S_k = (X_1, Y_1), ..., (X_k, Y_k)$ with $X_i \sim P(X|C_i)$. This trajectory is equivalent to the *support set* in MAML, as it mimics the non stationary learning conditions encountered at deployment time. Starting from initial parameters θ, we obtain *fast parameters* θ^k by processing the trajectory one (potentially batched) example at a time, performing k SGD steps, with loss $\ell(f_{\theta_i}(X_i), Y_i)$ at each inner step. Denoting the one-step SGD operator with learning rate α as

$$U(\theta^0) = \theta^0 - \alpha \nabla_{\theta^0} \ell_0(\theta^0, S_{[0]}) = \theta^1, \tag{2}$$

the *fast parameters* θ_k are given by

$$\theta^k = U \circ ... \circ U(\theta^0). \tag{3}$$

We proceed to evaluate parameters θ^k on a *query set* Q, obtaining the *outer loss* ℓ_{out}. We recall that two key properties of a continual learner are its ability to leverage past skills to quickly learn new concepts and to learn without negative interference on previous knowledge. To do so, the OML [21] objective insightfully proposes to compose Q with samples from current inner loop distribution $P(X|C_{i:k})$ but also from concepts seen in previous iterations of the pretraining phase, which we denote by C_{old}. The full objective can be written as

$$\min_\theta \sum_{C_{1:k} \sim p(\mathcal{C}^k)} \text{OML}(\theta) \overset{\text{def}}{=} \sum_{C_{1:k} \sim p(\mathcal{C}^k)} \sum_{S_k \sim p(S_k|C_{1:k})} \ell_{out}(U(\theta, S_k), Q) \tag{4}$$

Once ℓ_{out} has been evaluated, we backpropagate through the inner learning procedure, all the way to the initial θ. Using this gradient we calculate a new set of initial weights $\theta := U(\theta, \ell_{out})$ and iterate again over the whole process until convergence.

In practice, [21] partition the full model $f_\theta : \mathcal{X} \to \mathcal{Y}$ into a model base (or trunk) $b_{\theta_b} : \mathcal{X} \to \mathbb{R}^d$ which extracts a learned representation, and a model head $h_{\theta_h} : \mathbb{R}^d \to \mathcal{Y}$ which predicts the final output from the learned representation. In other words, the model can be represented as $f_\theta = h_{\theta_h} \circ b_{\theta_b}$. In practice, the network base typically contains all convolutional blocks, while the head is a small multi-layer perceptron.

During the inner loop (and deployment), only the head parameters θ_h are updated via SGD. The parameters θ_b are only updated in the outer loop, meaning that latent representations for all inputs can be extracted in parallel, since θ_b

is fixed. This modification also leads to training optimization procedure that is mode stable, leading to significantly better results.

Again, the key contribution of OML is that one can approximate the full $\mathcal{L}_{CLP}$ by artificially creating short non-stationary sequences and evaluating knowledge retention on a sample of past data. Crucially, the loss ℓ used in both inner and outer loop, is a supervised loss. Moreover, the non-stationary sequences are created using labelled information. In this work, we design a new algorithm for the pretraining phase which bypasses the need for labelled data. We discuss our approach next.

4 Proposed Method

In this section, we introduce the core components our method, SPeCiaL. We first discuss our unsupervised labelling procedure, enabling SPeCiaL to work on unlabelled datasets. We then discuss our mechanism to fight catastrophic forgetting. Lastly, we discuss several modifications reducing the computational and memory footprint of our method, a key requirement when scaling to larger datasets. A full workflow or our method is shown in Fig. 1.

4.1 Generating Pseudo Labels

Our labelling procedure relies on data augmentation in pixel space, in order to generate multiple transformed images, or views, that share common semantic features. Similar to instance-level classifiers, we propose to assign each image (and its generated views) to a unique label. However, unlike most instance-level classifiers, we do not require a large final linear layer, nor do we use noise contrastive estimation. Similar to OML, we reset class prototypes once their lifespan is complete, allowing for a tractable solution (more information in Sect. 4.3). We follow the augmentation pipeline described in [14], yielding a stochastic transformation operator consisting of three base augmentations: random cropping which is then resized back to the original size, random color distortions, and random Gaussian blur. We highlight that this procedure can operate online, meaning it does not require a separate isolated clustering step, as in [8,20]. Moreover, by incorporating the labelling procedure within our variant of OML, labels are not static, hence the model is less prone to overfitting, and can benefit from longer training (see Sect. 5.1).

4.2 Maximizing Parallel Computations

Processing the incoming batch of data sequentially hinders the ability to run computations in parallel. We make two modifications to circumvent this issue. First, following [7], we partition the full model such that the model head contains only the last linear classification layer. Since only the head parameters have to be executed sequentially, this enables us to run the feature extraction process in parallel, which represents a significant portion of the computation. Second, we train on *multiple sequences in parallel*. During the inner loop procedure, instead of processing a single example per timestep, we instead process M examples every step. This is equivalent to first generating M independent streams, and processing (in batch) one example per stream at each timestep. This further maximizes the proportion of parellizable operations. We refer to the number of sequences (M) in the inner loop as the *meta batch size*.

4.3 Delayed Feature Recall

The original OML objective proposes to sample across all previously seen contexts C_{old} (or previously seen classes) to obtain samples for the outer loop, such that the model is incentivized to learn an update procedure which is robust to forgetting. In our current framework, this is not currently possible as it would require to keep in memory a number of vectors in the output layer that is proportional to the number of images seen. Instead, we propose to sample only from the last N seen samples, by storing these recent samples in a queue. This way, only the output vectors of the samples in the queue need to be kept additionally in memory. As a consequence, the lifespan of a given label starts when an image first appears in the inner loop, and persists until the sample is fully discarded from the queue. Therefore, we only require that our model's output size be larger than the sum of the number of unique images seen within a meta-training step, and the queue size. We note that when sampling a random label for an incoming image, we make sure to exclude already assigned labels in the queue to avoid collisions.

Furthermore, instead of storing raw images in the queue, we instead store the representation produced by the model trunk $b : \mathcal{X} \to \mathbb{R}^d$. This reduces both the computational and memory footprint of our algorithm, since we are reusing previously computed features. We note that in practice, using a small queue works best. Therefore the representations are stored in the queue for a few iterations only, and do not become stale, so no additional mechanism to counter staleness [19] is needed. The full workflow of our method can be seen in Fig. 1.

5   Experiments

We design our experiments to evaluate how well the learned representations can transfer when learning new classes from a common domain.

Pretraining. In practice, for each meta-train step we instantiate a Continual Learning Problem as follows: we first sample a set of (e.g. 5) context variables $\{C_1, .., C_5\}$. From this set, we create a sequence of correlated contexts by repeating each context n times: $(C_1^{(1)}, \ldots, C_1^{(n)}, C_2^{(1)} \ldots, C_5^{(n)})$. In the supervised case, we create a context C_i for each distinct label Y_i in the meta-training set. Therefore, sampling from $P(X_i|C_i)$ is equivalent to sampling from the class-conditional

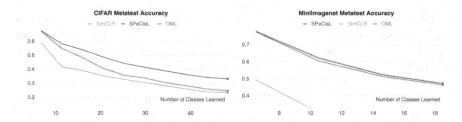

Fig. 2. MetaTest Accuracy during training of different models. Curves are averaged over three runs, and standard error is shaded. Smoothing is applied for clarity.

distribution $P(X_i|Y_i)$. For the unsupervised case, we create a context C_j for each image in the dataset, and sampling from $P(X_j|C_j)$ yields different augmented views of the j-th image in the meta-training set. For all methods considered, we cross validate the optimal value for the meta batch size.

Deployment: Few Shot Continual Learning. Following [7,8,21], our instantiation of a CLP follows the continual few shot learning procedure. At metatest time, we fix all layers except the last one (i.e. the RLN layers), as done in the inner loop procedure. We then proceed to learn a linear classifier (PLN) from a stream of C classes, with N_c samples for each class. The data is streamed example by example, one class at a time. In other words, the learner does $N_c \times C$ updates, seeing $N_c \times C$ samples (once), and observing $N_c - 1$ distribution shifts.

Datasets. We experiment on two datasets. We first employ the MiniImagenet [36] dataset, commonly used in few shot leaning. It comprises 100 classes, with 64 used for meta-training, 16 for meta-validation and 20 for meta-testing. Images are resized to 84×84. We also use the CIFAR-10/100 [24] datasets. All the meta-training is performed on CIFAR-10, and we do an 50-50 split for CIFAR100 for meta-validation and meta-test respectively. Images are resized to 32×32.

Architecture. For all baselines considered, we use a 4 block residual network. Each block consists of two computation paths, each with a single convolution. We use Weight Standardized [28] convolutions with Group Normalization [37], a normalization approach with does not use batch-level statistics and has shown strong performance in small batch settings. We use MaxPooling to downsample our input when required, i.e. in the all blocks for MiniImagenet, and the first three blocks for CIFAR. The block's architecture is illustrated in Fig. 3. The key difference with previous architectures commonly used in Meta Learning, is the use of a computational path with no activations. We further discuss the impact of these architectural changes in Sect. 5.2.

Baselines. We mainly compare against OML, where supervised pretraining is used. Our OML implementation can optionally leverage tools specific to the SSL pipeline, namely the use of augmentations. We also benchmark against SimCLR [14], a strong and flexible SSL model. For all approaches, we use the

Fig. 4. MetaTest Accuracy during training of different models. Curves are averaged over three runs, and standard error is shaded. Smoothing is applied for clarity.

same architecture and training budget, allowing us to compare methods on equal footing and better isolate the contribution of our method.

Pretraining. Models are trained for 350,000 optimization steps. For OML and SPeCiaL, a step corresponds to a full inner/outer loop, while for regular models it accounts for the processing of one minibatch. We found that for meta models, the AdamW optimizer with gradient clipping yielded best results. For other models, we used SGD with momentum. All models use a learning rate scheduler consisting of a linear warmup with cosine decay. For

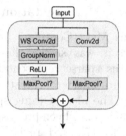

Fig. 3. Architecture Block. WS stands for Weight Standardized Convolutions. This block is used in the network base, denoted in red in Fig. 1 (Color figure online).

OML and SPeCiaL, we used cross-validation to determine the optimal sequence length, meta batch size and the number of distinct images per sequence. For SimCLR, we use the largest batch size which fits in memory, and the (batch size) adaptive learning rate procedure described in the paper. All experiments are executed on one Tesla V100 GPU.

MetaTesting. Once the models are trained, we evaluate their performance on the downstream Continual Few Shot Learning Task. As in [8, 21] we set the number of examples per class to 30. We follow [21] and cross-validate the learning rate for each metatest trajectory length reported.

5.1 Results

We first present results for the CIFAR experiment in Fig. 2. In this experiment, SPeCiaL is actually able to outperform its fully supervised counterpart. Moreover, this performance gap widens as more tasks are being learned, suggesting that the representations learned by our model are better adapted for longer (and more challenging) scenarios. We generally found that self supervised method, e.g.

SimcLR and SPeCiaL, can greatly benefit from longer training. Unlike OML, which starts overfitting after 100K steps, SPeCiaL continues to improve when given more computation. We illustrate this in Fig. 4. This observation is consistent with [6], who note that when combining supervised and SSL losses, after a fixed number of epochs the supervised signal needs to be removed to avoid a decrease in performance.

We proceed with the MiniImagenet experiment, shown on the right of Fig. 2. Here SPeCiaL is able to match the performance of OML. We note here that OML does not overfit as on the smaller scale CIFAR dataset. Instead, performance stagnates after 150K steps.

To summarize, early in training OML outperforms other unsupervised methods. As training progresses, SpeCiaL is able to close the performance gap, and benefits more from longer training.

5.2   Sparse Representation is Architecture-Dependent

In previous Meta Continual Learning paper, it was shown that the model learns sparse representations as a way to mitigate catastrophic forgetting. The idea of using sparse representations has been proposed in earlier work [17], and revisited in modern CL methods [4,25]. Therefore, seeing sparsity emerge in a data-driven way from MCL algorithms, as reported in [7,21], confirms that it is a good inductive bias for continual learning. In our work however, we found that the OML objective alone is not sufficient to obtain sparse representations: one must also use a suitable

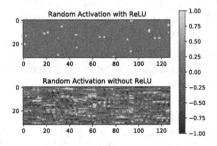

Fig. 5. Impact of ReLU activations on the sparsity of the learned representations. Bottom image shows a random representation obtained by our method, SPeCiaL, with the architecture presented above. Top picture is a random representation when we add a ReLU activation after the RLN output.

able architecture for sparsity to naturally emerge. In the original work, the architecture used consisted of Convolutions and ReLU activations, hence the last operation performed by the RLN was a nonlinearity favorable to cancelling neurons.

We run an experiment where we add an additional ReLU activation after the final block of the RLN. We compare the activations obtained with this variant in Fig. 5. We see that indeed sparsity emerges, which is not the case under the base architecture. Moreover, in the base architecture used in our experiments (see Fig. 3), one computational path finishes with a ReLU + MaxPool operation. Therefore the model could in practice only leverage this path and obtain sparse representations, without the explicit ReLU after the skip connection. Yet, we found that this skip connection is leveraged by the model, and overall stabilized training. We therefore conclude that the architecture used plays an important role in shaping the activation patterns. Moreover, we found that this additional

ReLU activation after the final skip connection gave a model which was harder to optimize, and therefore led to worse performance.

6 Conclusion

In this work we proposed a novel unsupervised meta objective to learn representations suitable for Continual Learning. We showed that when deployed in a Continual Learning setting, the learned representations can match or exceed the performance of fully supervised meta algorithms. Furthermore, we showed that sparsity does not always occur when using Meta Continual Learning algorithms, and that the architecture of the model plays a significant role in this context.

Our work takes a first step towards leveraging unlabelled data to prepare a system before its deployment on non-stationary data. An important next step for this work is to investigate how we can scale up meta algorithms presented in this work, and see if they can excel in the large data regime like Self-Supervised Learning methods.

References

1. Achille, A., et al.: Life-long disentangled representation learning with cross-domain latent homologies. arXiv preprint arXiv:1808.06508 (2018)
2. Aljundi, R., et al.: Online continual learning with maximally interfered retrieval. arXiv preprint arXiv:1908.04742 (2019)
3. Aljundi, R., Lin, M., Goujaud, B., Bengio, Y.: Gradient based sample selection for online continual learning. arXiv preprint arXiv:1903.08671 (2019)
4. Aljundi, R., Rohrbach, M., Tuytelaars, T.: Selfless sequential learning. arXiv preprint arXiv:1806.05421 (2018)
5. Antoniou, A., Storkey, A.: Assume, augment and learn: Unsupervised few-shot meta-learning via random labels and data augmentation. arXiv preprint arXiv:1902.09884 (2019)
6. Assran, M., Ballas, N., Castrejon, L., Rabbat, M.: Supervision accelerates pretraining in contrastive semi-supervised learning of visual representations. arXiv preprint arXiv:2006.10803 (2020)
7. Beaulieu, S., et al.: Learning to continually learn. arXiv preprint arXiv:2002.09571 (2020)
8. Bertugli, A., Vincenzi, S., Calderara, S., Passerini, A.: Generalising via meta-examples for continual learning in the wild. arXiv preprint arXiv:2101.12081 (2021)
9. Caccia, L., Belilovsky, E., Caccia, M., Pineau, J.: Online learned continual compression with adaptive quantization modules. In: International Conference on Machine Learning, pp. 1240–1250. PMLR (2020)
10. Caccia, M., et al.: Online fast adaptation and knowledge accumulation: a new approach to continual learning. arXiv preprint arXiv:2003.05856 (2020)
11. Caron, M., Misra, I., Mairal, J., Goyal, P., Bojanowski, P., Joulin, A.: Unsupervised learning of visual features by contrasting cluster assignments. arXiv preprint arXiv:2006.09882 (2020)
12. Chaudhry, A., Ranzato, M., Rohrbach, M., Elhoseiny, M.: Efficient lifelong learning with a-gem. arXiv preprint arXiv:1812.00420 (2018)

13. Chaudhry, A., et al.: Continual learning with tiny episodic memories (2019)
14. Chen, T., Kornblith, S., Norouzi, M., Hinton, G.: A simple framework for contrastive learning of visual representations. In: International Conference on Machine Learning, pp. 1597–1607. PMLR (2020)
15. Chen, X., Fan, H., Girshick, R., He, K.: Improved baselines with momentum contrastive learning. arXiv preprint arXiv:2003.04297 (2020)
16. Finn, C., Abbeel, P., Levine, S.: Model-agnostic meta-learning for fast adaptation of deep networks. In: International Conference on Machine Learning, pp. 1126–1135. PMLR (2017)
17. French, R.M.: Using semi-distributed representations to overcome catastrophic forgetting in connectionist networks. In: Proceedings of the 13th Annual Cognitive Science Society Conference, vol. 1, pp. 173–178 (1991)
18. Gupta, G., Yadav, K., Paull, L.: Look-ahead meta learning for continual learning. In: Larochelle, H., Ranzato, M., Hadsell, R., Balcan, M.F., Lin, H. (eds.) Advances in Neural Information Processing Systems, vol. 33, pp. 11588–11598. Curran Associates, Inc. (2020). https://proceedings.neurips.cc/paper/2020/file/85b9a5ac91cd629bd3afe396ec07270a-Paper.pdf
19. He, K., Fan, H., Wu, Y., Xie, S., Girshick, R.: Momentum contrast for unsupervised visual representation learning. In: Proceedings of the IEEE/CVF Conference on Computer Vision and Pattern Recognition, pp. 9729–9738 (2020)
20. Hsu, K., Levine, S., Finn, C.: Unsupervised learning via meta-learning. arXiv preprint arXiv:1810.02334 (2018)
21. Javed, K., White, M.: Meta-learning representations for continual learning. arXiv preprint arXiv:1905.12588 (2019)
22. Khodadadeh, S., Bölöni, L., Shah, M.: Unsupervised meta-learning for few-shot image classification. arXiv preprint arXiv:1811.11819 (2018)
23. Kirkpatrick, J., et al.: Overcoming catastrophic forgetting in neural networks. Proc. Natl. Acad. Sci. **114**(13), 3521–3526 (2017)
24. Krizhevsky, A., Hinton, G., et al.: Learning multiple layers of features from tiny images (2009)
25. Liu, V., Kumaraswamy, R., Le, L., White, M.: The utility of sparse representations for control in reinforcement learning. In: Proceedings of the AAAI Conference on Artificial Intelligence, vol. 33, pp. 4384–4391 (2019)
26. Lopez-Paz, D., Ranzato, M.: Gradient episodic memory for continual learning. arXiv preprint arXiv:1706.08840 (2017)
27. Nguyen, C.V., Li, Y., Bui, T.D., Turner, R.E.: Variational continual learning. arXiv preprint arXiv:1710.10628 (2017)
28. Qiao, S., Wang, H., Liu, C., Shen, W., Yuille, A.: Weight standardization. arXiv preprint arXiv:1903.10520 (2019)
29. Rao, D., Visin, F., Rusu, A.A., Teh, Y.W., Pascanu, R., Hadsell, R.: Continual unsupervised representation learning. arXiv preprint arXiv:1910.14481 (2019)
30. Ravi, S., Larochelle, H.: Optimization as a model for few-shot learning (2016)
31. Riemer, M., et al.: Learning to learn without forgetting by maximizing transfer and minimizing interference. arXiv preprint arXiv:1810.11910 (2018)
32. Shin, H., Lee, J.K., Kim, J., Kim, J.: Continual learning with deep generative replay. arXiv preprint arXiv:1705.08690 (2017)
33. Smith, J., Baer, S., Taylor, C., Dovrolis, C.: Unsupervised progressive learning and the STAM architecture. arXiv preprint arXiv:1904.02021 (2019)
34. Snell, J., Swersky, K., Zemel, R.S.: Prototypical networks for few-shot learning. arXiv preprint arXiv:1703.05175 (2017)

35. Van de Ven, G.M., Tolias, A.S.: Generative replay with feedback connections as a general strategy for continual learning. arXiv preprint arXiv:1809.10635 (2018)
36. Vinyals, O., Blundell, C., Lillicrap, T., Kavukcuoglu, K., Wierstra, D.: Matching networks for one shot learning. arXiv preprint arXiv:1606.04080 (2016)
37. Wu, Y., He, K.: Group normalization. In: Proceedings of the European Conference on Computer Vision (ECCV), pp. 3–19 (2018)
38. Zenke, F., Poole, B., Ganguli, S.: Continual learning through synaptic intelligence. In: International Conference on Machine Learning, pp. 3987–3995. PMLR (2017)

Distilled Replay: Overcoming Forgetting Through Synthetic Samples

Andrea Rosasco[1]([⊠])[iD], Antonio Carta[1][iD], Andrea Cossu[2][iD], Vincenzo Lomonaco[1][iD], and Davide Bacciu[1][iD]

[1] University of Pisa, Lungarno Antonio Pacinotti, 43, 56126 Pisa, PI, Italy
a.rosasco@studenti.unipi.it,
{antonio.carta,vincenzo.lomonaco,davide.bacciu}@unipi.it
[2] Scuola Normale Superiore, P.za dei Cavalieri, 7, 56126 Pisa, PI, Italy
andrea.cossu@sns.it

Abstract. Replay strategies are Continual Learning techniques which mitigate catastrophic forgetting by keeping a buffer of patterns from previous experiences, which are interleaved with new data during training. The amount of patterns stored in the buffer is a critical parameter which largely influences the final performance and the memory footprint of the approach. This work introduces Distilled Replay, a novel replay strategy for Continual Learning which is able to mitigate forgetting by keeping a very small buffer (1 pattern per class) of highly informative samples. Distilled Replay builds the buffer through a distillation process which compresses a large dataset into a tiny set of informative examples. We show the effectiveness of our Distilled Replay against popular replay-based strategies on four Continual Learning benchmarks.

Keywords: Continual learning · Distillation · Deep learning

1 Introduction

Deep learning models trained under the assumption that all training data is available from the beginning and each sample is independent and identically distributed manage to achieve impressive performance [14]. This learning scenario is often called *offline training*. Contrary to offline training, *continual learning* (CL) requires the model to learn sequentially from a stream of experiences [16]. Each experience is made of a batch of data, which may contain new knowledge such as novel classes that need to be distinguished by the model. Therefore, the model must be continually updated to incorporate knowledge coming from new experiences. However, when trained on new samples, neural networks tend to forget past knowledge: this phenomenon is called catastrophic forgetting [8]. Catastrophic forgetting emerges as a consequence of the stability-plasticity dilemma [10], that is the difficulty of a model to be both plastic enough to acquire new information and stable enough to preserve previously acquired knowledge.

Continual learning may have a large impact on a variety of real world applications: Computer vision [17], Natural Language Processing [23] and Robotics [24] are

F. Cuzzolin et al. (Eds.): CSSL 2021, LNAI 13418, pp. 104–117, 2022.
https://doi.org/10.1007/978-3-031-17587-9_8

examples of environments where the data is highly non stationary and may vary over time. A model able to learn continuously without forgetting would not need to be retrained from scratch every time a new experience is introduced (cumulative training). In fact, retraining is often the only viable alternative to continual learning in dynamic environments. However, retraining requires to store all the encountered data, which is often unfeasible under real world constraints. To address this problem, in this paper we focused on Replay strategies [1,5], a family of CL techniques which leverages a buffer of patterns from previous experiences and uses it together with the current data to train the model.

We introduce a novel CL strategy called Distilled Replay to address the problem of building very small replay buffers with highly informative samples. Distilled Replay is based on the assumption that, if a replay pattern represents most of the features present in a dataset, it will be more effective against forgetting than a randomly sampled pattern from the dataset. Moreover, keeping a small buffer is useful to deploy continual learning solutions in real-world applications, since the memory footprint is drastically reduced with respect to cumulative approaches. Distilled Replay directly optimizes the memory consumption by keeping a buffer of only one pattern per class, while still retaining most of the original performance. The buffer is built using a distillation process based on Dataset Distillation [27], which allows to condensate an entire dataset into few informative patterns. Dataset Distillation removes the need to select replay patterns from the real dataset. Instead, it learns patterns which summarize the main characteristics of the dataset. Distilled Replay acts by combining our modified version of Dataset Distillation with replay strategies. It shows that even one pattern per class is sufficient to mitigate forgetting. In contrast, other replay strategies need larger memory buffers to match the performance of our approach.

2 Continual Learning Scenario

In this work, we consider continual learning on a sequence of T experiences $E_1, \ldots, E_T$. Each experience E_t is associated to a training set D_t^{tr}, a validation set D_t^{vl} and a test set D_t^{ts}. A continual learning algorithm operating in the aforementioned scenario can be defined as follows [16]:

$$\forall D_t^{tr} \in S,$$
$$A_t^{CL} : \; <\boldsymbol{\theta}_{t-1}, D_t^{tr}, B_{t-1}, l_t> \; \rightarrow \; <\boldsymbol{\theta}_t, B_t>, \tag{1}$$

where:

- $\boldsymbol{\theta}_t$ are the model parameters at experience t, learned continually;
- B_t is an external buffer to store additional knowledge (like previously seen patterns);
- l_t is an optional task label associated to each experience. The task label can be used to disentangle tasks and customize the model parameters (e.g. by using multi-headed models [7]);
- D_t^{tr} is the training set of examples.

An algorithm respecting this formalization can be applied to different continual learning scenarios. In this paper, we used domain-incremental and class-incremental scenarios, identified in [26].

In Domain Incremental Learning (D-IL) the classes to learn are all present from the first experience, but their generating distribution is subjected to a drift from one experience to the other.

In Class Incremental Learning (C-IL) scenarios each experience provides patterns coming from classes which are not present in the other experiences.

We impose additional constraints to these scenarios, restricting the number of elements that can be stored from previous experiences to one per class and the number of epochs to one (single-pass).

3   Related Works

The challenge of learning continuously has been addressed from different point of views [16]. Regularization approaches try to influence the learning trajectory of a model in order to mitigate forgetting of previous knowledge [3]. The regularization term is designed to increase the model stability across multiple experiences, for example by penalizing large changes in parameters deemed important for previous experiences [13].

Architectural strategies refer to a large set of techniques aimed at dynamically modifying the model structure. The addition of new components (e.g. layers [21]) favors learning of new information, while forgetting can be mitigated by freezing previously added modules [2] or by allocating separate components without interference [6, 21].

3.1   Dual Memories Strategies

This family of CL algorithms is loosely inspired by the Complementary Learning System theory (CLS) [19]. This theory explains the memory consolidation process as the interplay between two structures: the hippocampus, responsible for the storage of recent episodic memories, and the neocortex, responsible for the storage of long-term knowledge and for the generalization to unseen events.

The idea of having an episodic memory (i.e. a buffer of previous patterns) which replays examples to a long-term storage (i.e. the model) is very popular in continual learning [5]. In fact, replay strategies are the most common representatives of dual memory strategies and very effective in class-incremental scenarios [25].

Replay strategies are based on a sampling operation, which extracts a small buffer of patterns from each experience, and on a training algorithm which combines examples from the buffer with examples from the current experience. Sampling policies may vary from random selection to the use of heuristics to select patterns that are more likely to improve recall of previous experiences [1]. Additionally, generative replay approaches [22] do not rely directly on patterns sampled from the dataset. Instead, they train a generative model to produce patterns similar to the ones seen at training time. Our approach share loose similarities with generative replay, since we do not replay patterns directly sampled from the original training set either. One important aspect of all replay approaches is the size of the replay buffer. Real-world applications may be constrained to the use of small buffers since they allow to scale to a large number of experiences. For this reason, one important objective of replay techniques is to minimize the buffer size [5]. However, relying on patterns sampled directly from the dataset or generated on-the-fly by a generative model may need many examples to mitigate forgetting. Our method, instead, leverages one of the simplest replay policies and manages to maintain one highly informative pattern per class in the buffer.

4 Distilled Replay

Our proposed approach, called Distilled Replay, belongs to the family of dual memory strategies. Distilled Replay combines a simple replay policy with a small buffer composed of highly informative patterns. Instead of using raw replay samples, Distilled Replay learns the patterns to be replayed via buffer distillation, a process based on dataset distillation [27]. In the remainder of this section, we describe the buffer distillation process and how to use it together with replay policies in continual learning.

4.1 Buffer Distillation

Replay strategies operating in the small buffer regime are forced to keep only few examples per class. These examples may not be representative of their own classes, thus reducing the effectiveness of the approach. Distilled Replay addresses this problem by implementing buffer distillation, a technique inspired by Dataset Distillation [27]. Our buffer distillation compresses a dataset into a small number of highly informative, synthetic examples. Given a dataset $x = \{x_i\}_{i=1}^N$, and an initialization θ_0, the goal is to learn a buffer of samples $\tilde{x} = \{\tilde{x}_i\}_{i=1}^M$, initialized with samples from the dataset, and with $M \ll N$. Performing S steps of SGD on the buffer $\tilde{x}$ results in a model

$$\theta_S = \theta_{S-1} - \eta \nabla_{\theta_{S-1}} \ell(\tilde{x}, \theta_{S-1}), \tag{2}$$

that performs well on the original dataset x. Buffer distillation achieves this result by solving the optimization problem:

$$\tilde{x}^* = \underset{\tilde{x}}{arg\,min} \ \mathbb{E}_{\theta_0 \sim p(\theta_0)} \sum_{s=1}^S \ell(x, \theta_S), \tag{3}$$

where $\ell(x, \theta)$ is the loss for model θ_S computed on x. We can solve the optimization problem defined in Eq. 3 by stochastic gradient descent (the dependence of Eq. 3 on $\tilde{x}$ is obtained by expanding θ_S as in Eq. 2). A model trained on synthetic samples $\tilde{x}^*$ reduces the prediction loss on the original training set. Moreover, using a distribution of initializations $p(\theta_0)$ makes the distilled samples independent from the specific model initialization values.

Algorithm 1 shows the pseudocode for buffer distillation. We refer to the loop that updates the distilled images as outer loop and to the one that updates the model as inner loop.

Our buffer distillation has some distinguishing characteristics with respect to the original Dataset Distillation [27].

While Dataset Distillation learns the learning rate η used in the inner loop, we decided to fix it. In fact, Distilled Replay, during training, uses the same learning rate for past and current examples. If the examples were distilled to work with custom learning rates, they would lose their effectiveness when used with a different one. Therefore, during distillation the learning rate is the same used by the model during continual learning.

Another important difference with respect to Dataset Distillation is that our approach uses a different loss function. Instead of measuring the loss of the model on a minibatch of training data on the inner last step, our algorithm does that at each steps and backpropagate on their sum. As a result, buffer distillation is equivalent to backpropagating the gradient at each inner step and then updating the distilled images once the inner training is over. This process is graphically described by Fig. 1

We can summarize our buffer distillation in three steps:

1. Do S steps of gradient descent on the distilled images, obtaining $\boldsymbol{\theta}_1, \ldots, \boldsymbol{\theta}_S$.
2. Evaluate each model on a minibatch of training data x_t getting the loss $L_{tot} = \sum_{i=1}^{S} \ell(x_r, \boldsymbol{\theta}_i)$.
3. Compute $\nabla_{\tilde{x}} L_{tot}$ and update the distilled images.

Algorithm 1. Buffer Distillation

Input: $p(\boldsymbol{\theta}_0)$: distribution of initial weights; M: number of distilled samples
Input: α: step size; R: number of outer steps; η: learning rate
Input: S: number of inner inner steps.

1: Initialize $\tilde{x} = \{\tilde{x}_i\}_{i=1}^{M}$
2: **for all** outer steps $r = 1$ **to** R **do**
3:     Get a minibatch of real training data $x_r = \{x_j\}_{j=1}^{n}$
4:     Sample a batch of initial weights $\boldsymbol{\theta}_0^{(j)} \sim p(\boldsymbol{\theta}_0)$
5:     **for all** sampled $\boldsymbol{\theta}_0^{(j)}$ **do**
6:         **for all** inner steps $s = 1$ **to** S **do**
7:             Compute updated parameter with GD: $\boldsymbol{\theta}_s^{(j)} = \boldsymbol{\theta}_{s-1}^{(j)} - \eta \nabla_{\boldsymbol{\theta}_{s-1}^{(j)}} \ell(\tilde{x}, \boldsymbol{\theta}_{s-1}^{(j)})$
8:             Evaluate the objective function on real training data: $\mathcal{L}^{(s,j)} = \ell(x_r, \boldsymbol{\theta}_s^{(j)})$
9:         **end for**
10:    **end for**
11:    Update $\tilde{x} \leftarrow \tilde{x} - \alpha \nabla_{\tilde{x}} \sum_s \sum_j \mathcal{L}^{(s,j)}$
12: **end for**
Output: distilled data $\tilde{x}$

4.2 Distilled Replay Training

Distilled Replay combines a replay policy with the buffer learned by buffer distillation and is designed to work with very small buffers, comprising as little as a single pattern per class.

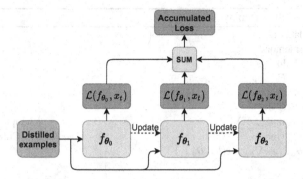

Fig. 1. Schematic representation of Buffer Distillation update. The gradient is backpropagated to the distilled examples following the computation path defined by the solid arrows. The accumulated loss sums the loss computed on each step.

During training, the replay policy builds each minibatch with elements sampled from the current dataset D_t^{tr} and patterns from the buffer B_t. The combination of old and new data allows the model to learn the current experience while mitigating forgetting on past ones.

At the end of the t-th experience, we randomly sample a certain amount of elements per class from the current training set and use them to initialise the memory m_t. We then apply buffer distillation to learn the synthetic memory $\tilde{m}_t$. Finally, as shown in Fig. 2, we add the distillation result to the distilled buffer. Algorithm 2 shows the pseudocode for the entire training loop.

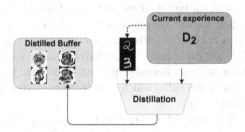

Fig. 2. On experience t, a set of training examples is sampled from the current dataset, distilled and added to the buffer. The distilled samples will then be replayed alongside the next experience dataset.

5   Experiments

We used average accuracy [4] as the main metric to monitor forgetting of previous knowledge. After training on the t-th experience, the average accuracy is evaluated by averaging on all experiences encountered so far:

$$\mathcal{A}_t = \frac{1}{t} \sum_{i=1}^{t} A(\boldsymbol{\theta}, D_i), \tag{4}$$

Algorithm 2. Distilled Replay Training

1: $v \leftarrow$ list of datasets
2: $B_0 \leftarrow$ list of memories
3: **for** $t = 1$ **to** T **do**
4:     $D_t^{tr}, D_t^{ts} \sim E_t$
5:     $v.\text{insert}(D_t^{ts})$
6:     **for** $q = 1$ **to** Q **do**
7:         $\text{mb}_q = \text{sample}(D_t^{tr})$ {Sample from dataset}
8:         $b_q = B_t \cup \text{mb}_q$ {Create minibatch}
9:         $\boldsymbol{\theta}_q \leftarrow \boldsymbol{\theta}_{q-1} - \nabla_{\boldsymbol{\theta}_{q-1}} \ell(b_q, \boldsymbol{\theta}_{q-1})$
10:     **end for**
11:     $m_t \sim D_t^{tr}$
12:     $\tilde{m}_t \leftarrow \text{buffer distillation}(m_t, D_t^{tr})$
13:     $B_t \leftarrow B_{t-1} \cup \tilde{m}_t$
14:     **for all** D_i^{ts} in v **do**
15:         $\text{test}(\boldsymbol{\theta}_Q, D_i^{ts})$
16:     **end for**
17: **end for**

---

where $\mathcal{A}(\boldsymbol{\theta}, D_i)$ is the accuracy on dataset D_i from experience E_i obtained with a model parameterized by $\boldsymbol{\theta}$.

We compared our approach against 5 different continual learning strategies:

Naive (LB) trains the model continually without taking any measure to prevent forgetting. We use this strategy as a Lower Bound (LB) for continual learning performance.

Simple Replay (SR) stores a buffer of examples randomly extracted from previous datasets and uses them to rehearse previous experiences.

Cumulative (UB) trains the model continually on the union of the datasets from the current and all the past experiences. Cumulative training keeps all the past data. Therefore, we used it as Upper Bound (UB) for the continual learning performance.

iCaRL [20] a dual-memory algorithm which combines knowledge distillation and nearest class mean classification.

Maximal Interfered Retrieval (MIR) [1] a dual-memory algorithm which selects the samples to be replayed based on how much their accuracy would drop after a training step on the current minibatch of data.

We measured the ability of the six strategies to prevent forgetting by using a single sample per class. We used a Multilayer Perceptron with one hidden layer of 500 units in the D-IL scenario and a LeNet5 [15] in the C-IL scenario.

Table 1. Average accuracies of the six tested methods on the four benchmarks. The leftmost column of each table reports the experience up to which the accuracy is averaged. For Permuted MNIST, we report the average accuracy starting from the 6-th experience. In fact, the last experiences better represents the overall performance, since the accuracy is averaged over all experiences seen so far.

	UB	LB	DR	SR	iCaRL	MIR
E_6	.96	.91	**.93**	.91	.92	.91
E_7	.96	.89	**.92**	.90	.91	.90
E_8	.96	.87	**.91**	.88	.90	.89
E_9	.96	.84	**.91**	.88	.89	.85
E_{10}	.97	.83	**.90**	.88	.89	.83

(a) Permuted MNIST

	UB	LB	DR	SR	iCaRL	MIR
E_2	.96	.49	**.93**	.88	.91	.92
E_3	.94	.33	**.89**	.70	.85	.78
E_4	.93	.25	**.87**	.66	.81	.68
E_5	.91	.20	**.82**	.61	.77	.59

(b) Split MNIST

	UB	LB	DR	SR	iCaRL	MIR
E_2	.93	.50	**.84**	.74	.82	.76
E_3	.84	.33	**.67**	.55	.66	.55
E_4	.76	.30	**.63**	.54	.59	.55
E_5	.78	.19	**.63**	.48	.60	.45

(c) Split Fashion MNIST

	UB	LB	DR	SR	iCaRL	MIR
E_2	.56	.28	**.52**	.43	.41	.49
E_3	.43	.21	**.34**	.29	.29	.32
E_4	.38	.18	**.28**	.21	.23	.18
E_5	.35	.14	**.24**	.19	21	.19

(d) Split CIFAR-10

We experimented with four popular continual learning benchmarks for image classification: Permuted MNIST [9], Split MNIST [29], Split Fashion MNIST [28] and Split CIFAR10 [18].

Permuted MNIST is a Domain-incremental scenario in which each experience is constructed by applying a fixed random permutation to all the MNIST images. The permutation only changes at the end of each experience. We used 10 experiences in total. The other benchmarks are class-incremental benchmarks in which each experience is composed by examples from two classes. In this setup, the number of classes increases every time a new experience is introduced. Therefore, the number of experiences is 5 for each benchmark.

5.1 Results

Table 1 reports the average accuracy after training on each experience for all the evaluated strategies. Distilled Replay consistently outperforms the other methods, often by a large margin. In particular, neither iCaRL nor MIR are able to surpass Distilled Replay in the challenging continual learning scenario used in our experiments (single-epoch, replay buffers with one pattern per class). On Permuted MNIST, after the last experience, the accuracies of the compared methods drop between 83% and 89%. Our Distilled Replay is able to reach around 90% accuracy at the end of the last experience.

In C-IL benchmarks, Distilled Replay outperforms the other strategies by a larger margins than in the D-IL scenario. Table 1b shows the performance on Split MNIST.

iCaRL and MIR obtained 77% and 59% accuracy respectively, while Distilled Replay achieves an accuracy of 82%. Figure 4 shows the patterns in the replay buffer of Simple Replay and Distilled Replay. The ones used by standard replay are simply patterns taken from the training datasets. The patterns in the buffer of Distilled Replay shows a white background and a thicker digit contour. The performance of Distilled Replay and Simple Replay differs not only in accuracy values but also in their trajectories: Simple Replay accuracy degrades faster as the training progresses. To highlight this phenomenon, Fig. 3 reports the accuracies on each experience throughout learning. We can see how dataset distillation maintains a higher accuracy on past experiences. This results in a more stable average accuracy.

More challenging C-IL benchmarks such as Split Fashion MNIST (Table 1c) and Split CIFAR-10 (Table 1d) show similar differences between Distilled replay performances and the ones of the compared strategies. Distilled Replay outperforms the other methods, but the absolute performance of all six strategies is lower than on Split MNIST.

From Table 1d, we can observe that on Split CIFAR-10 there is a large drop in performance compared to the previous benchmarks. This is consistent for all the evaluated strategies. In Sect. 6 we highlight some of the issues that may explain the reduced performance of Distilled Replay on challenging data consisting of complex patterns.

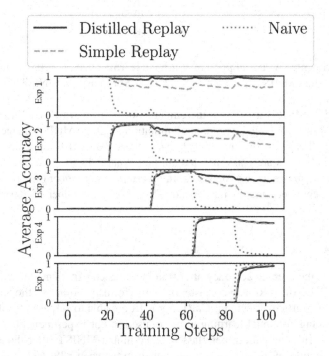

Fig. 3. Accuracies on each S-MNIST experience. Without replaying any data, the performance on previous experiences drop. By using distilled replay, we manage to get higher performance compared to standard replay.

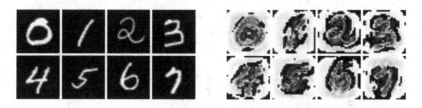

Fig. 4. Replay memory content of Simple Replay (left) and Distilled Replay (right). Distilled samples highlight the most representative features of the input patterns.

5.2 Ablation Study

Our buffer distillation process introduces significant differences as compared to the original Dataset Distillation technique [27] (see Sect. 4). Therefore, we ran experiments on Split MNIST to validate the importance of these modifications in a continual learning scenario. The hyperparameters have been selected as follows. We kept the same number of inner and outer steps of distillation in both algorithms, so that the computation time is approximately equal. Instead, the learning rate of the outer update was selected by validating on different values (i.e. 0.05, 0.1, 0.5). In particular, we found that increasing the outer learning rates from 0.1 to 0.5 led to a better performance in Dataset Distillation.

Figure 5 shows the learning curves of the Dataset Distillation and Buffer Distillation techniques. As soon as the model starts learning on the second experience, our distillation process outperforms Dataset Distillation, supporting the observation that the distilled samples have higher quality.

5.3 Computational Times

The Buffer Distillation process scales linearly with the number of inner steps. In a continual learning setting, we continually adapt the model and, consequently, the buffer. This requires the model to be able to learn from multiple passes over data. Therefore, we experimented with large values for the inner steps. However, the high number of steps in the inner loop contributed to increase the computational cost of the distillation. Notice that, differently from other popular continual learning strategies (e.g. GEM [18]), whose computation mainly occurs during continual training, the distillation process is independent of the training on the current experience. Therefore, it is possible to perform Buffer Distillation in parallel to training as soon as a new experience arrives. Figure 6 reports the average time of the distillation process executed on a GPU Nvidia V100. The data comes from the distillation of Split CIFAR-10 experiences. In our experiments, the best configurations in terms of final average accuracy used 80 outer steps and 20 inner steps, with an average time of 38 minutes for each buffer distillation. While this is not a prohibitive amount of computational time, it has to be multiplied by the number of experiences in the stream (except for the last one which is not distilled), making the Distilled Replay a relatively expensive strategy in terms of computational times.

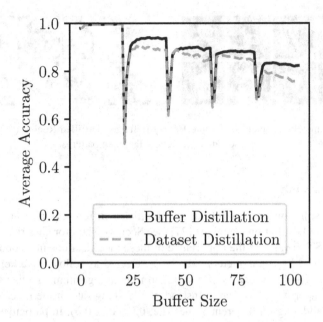

Fig. 5. Comparison of two versions of the distilled replay algorithm on Split MNIST. One version is based on the original Dataset Distillation algorithm [27], while the other uses our buffer distillation.

6   Discussion

The main objective of our experimental analysis was to test whether replay strategies with small buffers of one pattern per class were able to mitigate forgetting.[1] The results show that, in this small buffer regime, the use of real patterns sampled from the dataset may not be sufficient to recover performance of previous experiences. Instead, we show that highly informative samples generated by Buffer Distillation allow to mitigate forgetting. Building on our results, we can also identify some additional insights and issues of Distilled Replay worth exploring in further developments.

Independence of Distillation Processes. Since the buffer distillation process is applied separately for each experience, the synthetic samples are optimized without taking into account previous (and future) experiences. This makes the distillation process easier but it also brings possible downsides. For example, distilling samples of similar classes belonging to different experiences may introduce ambiguous features and increase the forgetting on such classes. Since we keep a single example per class, similar samples of different classes would negatively impact the final accuracy. Datasets such as Fashion MNIST, containing a high number of classes similar to each other (e.g. t-shirt, shirt, coat, dress, pullover), may be affected by this problem.

---

[1] The code along with the configuration files needed to reproduce our results are available at https://github.com/andrearosasco/DistilledReplay.

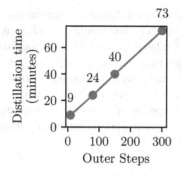
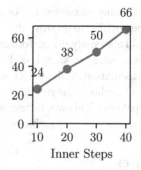

Fig. 6. Average time for a single buffer distillation on Split CIFAR10. On the left, we show the time as a function of the number of outer steps (inner steps fixed to 10). On the right, we show the time as a function of the inner steps (outer steps fixed to 80).

Distilled Replay with Complex Architectures. The results we showed for C-IL benchmarks use a LeNet5 architecture [15]. To improve the results on S-CIFAR-10 we did some preliminary experiments using a ResNet architecture [11] together with Distilled Replay. However, we were not able to distill useful samples. The results (not shown in the paper) suggest that the buffer distillation process struggles with more complex architectures. We hypothesize that the optimization of the distilled examples is too challenging for gradient descent on sufficiently complex models. In fact, the distillation objective requires the backpropagation of the gradient through multiple gradient descent steps. For sufficiently complex architectures, this would result in a large computational graph which may suffer from vanishing or exploding gradients issues [12].

Robustness to Continual Training. Buffer Distillation is able to learn robust samples which better mitigate forgetting than the ones generated by the original Dataset Distillation. This is mainly due to the fact that buffer distillation optimizes the loss for each point of the learning trajectory. Therefore, the outer updates takes into consideration to what extent each distilled image influences the learning trajectory of the model. As a result, buffer distillation produces patterns which are robust to small parameter changes. This is important in a continual learning setting, where the model must continually adapt to novel experiences.

7   Conclusion and Future Work

Replay based methods are among the most effective continual learning strategies. In this work, we introduced a novel replay strategy called Distilled Replay which combines replay with Buffer Distillation, a process that generates a small buffer of highly informative samples. In particular, we studied whether keeping in the buffer a single pattern per class is sufficient to recover most of the original performance. When compared to other replay strategies like iCaRL and MIR, Distilled Replay shows superior results. The ability of Buffer Distillation to learn highly informative patterns is crucial to boost the performance of replay with small buffers.

By leveraging recent works about novel dataset condensation mechanisms [30, 31], it would be possible to improve the computational efficiency of Distilled Replay. Future works could also study the performance of Distilled Replay in very constrained settings where it is required to store less than one pattern per class, for example by iteratively applying distillation on the buffer itself. Ultimately, we hope that our work will foster the study of replay strategies in the small buffer regime, where it is only possible to store few patterns. This would help in the development of more efficient and sustainable continual learning systems, able to operate in the real-world constrained settings.

References

1. Aljundi, R., et al.: Online continual learning with maximal interfered retrieval. Adv. Neural Inf. Process. Syst. **32**, 11849–11860 (2019)
2. Asghar, N., Mou, L., Selby, K.A., Pantasdo, K.D., Poupart, P., Jiang, X.: Progressive memory banks for incremental domain adaptation. In: International Conference on Learning Representations (2019)
3. Chaudhry, A., Dokania, P.K., Ajanthan, T., Torr, P.H.S.: Riemannian walk for incremental learning: understanding forgetting and intransigence. In: Ferrari, V., Hebert, M., Sminchisescu, C., Weiss, Y. (eds.) ECCV 2018. LNCS, vol. 11215, pp. 556–572. Springer, Cham (2018). https://doi.org/10.1007/978-3-030-01252-6_33
4. Chaudhry, A., Ranzato, M., Rohrbach, M., Elhoseiny, M.: Efficient lifelong learning with A-GEM. In: ICLR (2019)
5. Chaudhry, A., et al.: On Tiny Episodic Memories in Continual Learning. arXiv (2019)
6. Cossu, A., Carta, A., Bacciu, D.: Continual learning with gated incremental memories for sequential data processing. In: Proceedings of the 2020 International Joint Conference on Neural Networks (IJCNN 2020) (2020). https://doi.org/10.1109/ijcnn48605.2020.9207550
7. Farquhar, S., Gal, Y.: Towards robust evaluations of continual learning. In: Privacy in Machine Learning and Artificial Intelligence Workshop, ICML (2019)
8. French, R.M.: Catastrophic forgetting in connectionist networks. Trends Cogn. Sci. **3**, 128–135 (1999). https://doi.org/10.1016/S1364-6613(99)01294-2
9. Goodfellow, I.J., Mirza, M., Xiao, D., Courville, A., Bengio, Y.: An empirical investigation of catastrophic forgetting in gradient-based neural networks (2015)
10. Grossberg, S.: How does a brain build a cognitive code? Psychol. Rev. **87**(1), 1–51 (1980). https://doi.org/10.1037/0033-295X.87.1.1
11. He, K., Zhang, X., Ren, S., Sun, J.: Deep residual learning for image recognition. In: 2016 IEEE Conference on Computer Vision and Pattern Recognition (CVPR), pp. 770–778 (2016). https://doi.org/10.1109/CVPR.2016.90
12. Hochreiter, S.: Untersuchungen zu dynamischen neuronalen netzen (1991)
13. Kirkpatrick, J., et al.: Overcoming catastrophic forgetting in neural networks. PNAS **114**(13), 3521–3526 (2017)
14. Krizhevsky, A., Sutskever, I., Hinton, G.E.: ImageNet classification with deep convolutional neural networks. In: Pereira, F., Burges, C.J.C., Bottou, L., Weinberger, K.Q. (eds.) Advances in Neural Information Processing Systems, vol. 25. Curran Associates, Inc. (2012). https://doi.org/10.1145/3065386
15. LeCun, Y., Bottou, L., Bengio, Y., Haffner, P.: Gradient-based learning applied to document recognition. Proc. IEEE **86**, 2278–2323 (1998). https://doi.org/10.1109/5.726791
16. Lesort, T., et al.: Continual learning for robotics: definition, framework, learning strategies, opportunities and challenges. Inf. Fusion. **58**, 52–68 (2020). https://doi.org/10.1016/j.inffus.2019.12.004

17. Lomonaco, V., Maltoni, D.: CORe50: a new dataset and benchmark for continuous object recognition. In: Proceedings of the 1st Annual Conference on Robot Learning, vol. 78, pp. 17–26 (2017)
18. Lopez-Paz, D., Ranzato, M.: Gradient episodic memory for continual learning. Adv. Neural Inf. Process. Syst. **30**, 6468–6477 (2017)
19. McClelland, J.L., McNaughton, B.L., O'Reilly, R.C.: Why there are complementary learning systems in the hippocampus and neocortex: insights from the successes and failures of connectionist models of learning and memory. Psychol. Rev. **102**, 419–457 (1995). https://doi.org/10.1037/0033-295X.102.3.419
20. Rebuffi, S.A., Kolesnikov, A., Sperl, G., Lampert, C.H.: iCaRL: incremental classifier and representation learning. In: The IEEE Conference on Computer Vision and Pattern Recognition (CVPR) (2017). https://doi.org/10.1109/cvpr.2017.587
21. Rusu, A.A., et al.: Progressive Neural Networks. arXiv (2016)
22. Shin, H., Lee, J.K., Kim, J., Kim, J.: Continual learning with deep generative replay. In: Guyon, I., (eds.) et al. Advances in Neural Information Processing Systems, vol. 30, pp. 2990–2999. Curran Associates, Inc. (2017)
23. Sun, F.K., Ho, C.H., Lee, H.Y.: LAMOL: LAnguage MOdeling for Lifelong Language Learning. In: ICLR (2020)
24. Thrun, S.: A lifelong learning perspective for mobile robot control. In: Graefe, V. (ed.) Intelligent Robots and Systems, pp. 201–214. Elsevier Science B.V., Amsterdam (1995). https://doi.org/10.1016/B978-044482250-5/50015-3
25. van de Ven, G.M., Siegelmann, H.T., Tolias, A.S.: Brain-inspired replay for continual learning with artificial neural networks. Nat. Commun. **11**, 4069 (2020). https://doi.org/10.1038/s41467-020-17866-2
26. van de Ven, G.M., Tolias, A.S.: Three scenarios for continual learning. arXiv (2019)
27. Wang, T., Zhu, J.Y., Torralba, A., Efros, A.A.: Dataset distillation. arXiv (2018)
28. Xiao, H., Rasul, K., Vollgraf, R.: Fashion-MNIST: a novel image dataset for benchmarking machine learning algorithms. arXiv (2017)
29. Zenke, F., Poole, B., Ganguli, S.: Continual learning through synaptic intelligence. In: International Conference on Machine Learning, pp. 3987–3995 (2017)
30. Zhao, B., Bilen, H.: Dataset condensation with differentiable Siamese augmentation (2021)
31. Zhao, B., Mopuri, K.R., Bilen, H.: Dataset condensation with gradient matching (2021)

Self-supervised Novelty Detection for Continual Learning: A Gradient-Based Approach Boosted by Binary Classification

Jingbo Sun[1]([✉]) [iD], Li Yang[1] [iD], Jiaxin Zhang[2] [iD], Frank Liu[2] [iD],
Mahantesh Halappanavar[3] [iD], Deliang Fan[1] [iD], and Yu Cao[1] [iD]

[1] Arizona State University, Tempe, USA
{jsun127,lyang166,dfan,Yu.Cao}@asu.edu
[2] Oak Ridge National Laboratory, Oak Ridge, USA
{zhangj,liufy}@ornl.gov
[3] Pacific Northwest National Laboratory, Richland, USA
Mahantesh.Halappanavar@pnnl.gov

Abstract. Novelty detection aims to automatically identify out of distribution (OOD) data, without any prior knowledge of them. It is a critical step in continual learning, in order to sense the arrival of new data and initialize the learning process. Conventional methods of OOD detection perform multi-variate analysis on an ensemble of data or features, and usually resort to the supervision with OOD data to improve the accuracy. In reality, such supervision is impractical as one cannot anticipate the anomalous data. In this paper, we propose a novel, self-supervised approach that does not rely on any pre-defined OOD data: (1) The new method evaluates the Mahalanobis distance of the gradients between the in-distribution and OOD data. (2) It is assisted by a self-supervised binary classifier to guide the label selection to generate the gradients, and maximize the Mahalanobis distance. In the evaluation with multiple datasets, such as CIFAR-10, CIFAR-100, SVHN and ImageNet, the proposed approach consistently outperforms state-of-the-art supervised and unsupervised methods in the area under the receiver operating characteristic (AUROC). We further demonstrate that this detector is able to accurately learn one OOD class in continual learning.

Keywords: Novelty detection · Continual learning · Mahalanobis distance · Unsupervised learning

1 Introduction

Deep neural networks (DNNs) have achieved high accuracy in many fields, such as image classification, natural language processing, and speech recognition. Their success is built upon carefully handcrafted DNN architectures, big data collection and expensive model training. A well-trained model promises high

F. Cuzzolin et al. (Eds.): CSSL 2021, LNAI 13418, pp. 118–133, 2022.
https://doi.org/10.1007/978-3-031-17587-9_9

inference accuracy if the input falls into the distribution of the training data. However, in many real-world scenarios, there is no guarantee that the input is always in the distribution. The encounter with out-of-distribution (OOD) input is inevitable due to the difficulty in data collection, unforeseeable user scenarios, and complex dynamics.

To manage the emergence of OOD data at the first moment, it is vitally important to have an accurate novelty detector that continuously evaluates the data stream and alarms the system once OOD data arrives. Upon the detection of OOD arrival, the system can then manage the situation with three possible methods: (1) It can rely on the OOD detector to collect new data and send them back to the data center, such that OOD data can be combined with previous in-distribution data (IDD) to re-train the model; (2) It can temporally utilize the detector as a one-class classifier to recognize the new class of OOD, in addition to existing IDD classes; and (3) It can activate a continual learning method at the edge to adapt the model in the field, such as the multi-head method with the assistance of the OOD detector. In all three cases, the accuracy and robustness of the novelty detector guard the success of continual model adaptation and knowledge update.

In this work, we propose a self-supervised approach which generates a set of OOD data from unsupervised statistical analysis, instead of supervised labeling. This set of OOD data is then combined with IDD data to train a binary classifier, which in turn, helps boost the performance of the unsupervised detector that collects more OOD data for training. As this mutual process continues, our novelty detector achieves higher and higher confidence in OOD detection. The contributions of this paper are as follows:

- Gradient-based novelty detection that employs the Mahalanobis distance as the metric to differentiate in-distribution and OOD input. The gradients are generated from a pre-trained classifier for IDD only, without any pre-knowledge of OOD.
- A self-supervised binary classifier. As previous works demonstrated, the availability of a binary classifier helps boost the accuracy. Yet distinguished from them, we don't rely on any labelled OOD data to train the classifier. The training set is initialized by the gradient-based detector. In turn, the binary classifier pre-screens OOD and IDD, and guides the selection of labels in the gradient-based detector to maximize the distance calculation. Through such mutual assistance, our approach is unsupervised and continually improves the accuracy.
- High accuracy in OOD detection and one-class classification. We evaluate our methodology in a comprehensive set of benchmarks. Our self-supervised method consistently achieves higher AUROC than other supervised and unsupervised results, confirming the advantages in gradient-based novelty detection.

2   Previous Works on Novelty Detection

Current OOD detectors usually use the information extracted from either the data itself or features projected by the feedforward path in the IDD engine. [7] demonstrated that the softmax score of the outlier tended to be higher compared with IDD and thus, thresholding inputs based on this score is feasible to detect the OOD. [13] improved this idea by introducing input preprocessing and temperature scaling. [12] proved that the in-distribution samples formed a multivariate Gaussian distribution in the high dimensional feature space, and proposed to use the Mahalanobis distance to measure how far an outlier is away from this in-distribution. There also exist autoencoder based OOD detectors [1,2,5,10,19,24] which use the reconstruction loss from the decoder to characterize the novelty. These data or activation-based methods demonstrated the value in OOD detection. On the other side, they have not explored one important step in the development of DNNs, the gradients back-propagated from the classification layer. These gradients present the first-order derivative to adapt the model and improve the separation of multiple classes. They contain a rich body of information to differentiate OOD from IDD.

To collect the gradients from the classifier that is prepared for the IDD, a label is required for cross-entropy loss and back-propagation. However, one challenge in the gradient-based approach is that labels of OOD data are not available in the process of novelty detection. To address this issue, a recent work by [11] introduced the confounding label, which only triggers small gradients for the IDD input. The gradients of the OOD input would be larger since they introduce many new features that are different from IDD. [10] explored the gradient-based representations of the novelty but they avoid the label issue by proposing a directional gradient constraint to the loss function so that the gradient direction of the OOD input does not align with the ones of the IDD. However, this method requires re-training of the model. In contrast, in this work, we utilize the gradient-based approach and the pre-trained model without any modification. In addition, we only use the training labels to collect the gradient.

Note that to boost the accuracy in novelty detection, many prior approaches utilize supervised training. They adopted a small amount of OOD samples to pre-train the novelty detector. For example, [12] trained a logistic regression detector to estimate the weights for feature ensemble. [11] trained a binary detector to distinguish the gradient representation of the in-distribution and OOD input. However, this type of supervised training requires the availability of labelled OOD data up front, which restricts its application in reality.

3   Proposed Methodology

The overarching goal of our methodology is to accurately identify OOD data from IDD. A successful OOD detection is equivalent to correctly classify the OOD input as one new class (i.e., one-class classification). For IDD inputs, they will be classified to the previous known classes. To achieve this goal, we propose a closed-loop methodology that interleaves the unsupervised ODD detector based on the

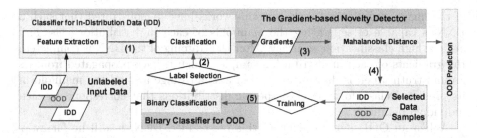

Fig. 1. The flow of our self-supervised OOD detector. (1) A DNN-based classifier is first prepared for IDD data. (2) The binary classifier predicts IDD or OOD. If the result is OOD, then in the IDD classifier, it selects the appropriate label to maximize the distance. (3) Based on the selected label, gradients are generated by the IDD classifier for the calculation of Mahalanobis distance. (4) From each patch of data, a balanced set of IDD and OOD data is selected based on the Mahalanobis distance. (5) This balanced IDD/OOD data set is used to continuously train the binary classifier.

Mahalanobis distance, with a binary IDD/OOD classifier. Figure 1 illustrates our methodology, consisting of these two main components:

- A gradient-based novelty detector: Distinguished from previous works that analyzed either the input data or the features, our detector exploits the gradients propagated backward from the classification layer for statistical analysis. The classifier in this step is designed for IDD only and all labels are from the IDD classes. To maximize the Mahalanobis distance between OOD and IDD classes, we select the appropriate class to label the OOD data, which is predicted by a binary classifier, as in Fig. 1.
- A self-supervised binary classifier. This classifier is designed to pre-screen IDD and OOD data, in order to assist label selection to generate the gradients. While the structure of this binary classifier is similar as that in [4], the training does not rely on any labeled data, but from a balanced set that is selected by the detector based on the Mahalanobis distance.

Overall, the mutual assistance between these two components helps accomplish OOD detection without the need of external supervision. In the following subsections, we first introduce our main processing path in OOD detection: the Mahalanobis distance in the gradient space. We then introduce the binary classifier as a necessary assistant to boost the performance of the main path, as well as the self-supervised training of it. Finally, we describe how these two components mutually assist each other with a thorough case study.

3.1 Gradient-Based Novelty Detector

Our approach starts from a given dataset of in-distribution data (IDD), and a deep neural network (DNN) based classifier trained by this IDD dataset. Note that at this step, only labels for IDD classes are accessible. In our examples of the image classification task, previous works have demonstrated that such a DNN is capable of separating the manifolds of each in-distribution class and achieve high classification accuracy. After the training of the DNN is completed, the gradients of each in-distribution sample, which is back-propagated from its ground-truth label, is distributed within a small range around the manifold of its predicted class, forming class-specific distributions that correspond to each individual manifold.

When an OOD data is given to this pre-trained DNN, it will lie far away from any manifold of IDD. Without any knowledge about this OOD data, if we still perform gradient-based training supervised by the IDD label, the DNN model will experience much larger gradients which force the model to reconstruct itself toward the OOD data. In this context, the distribution of gradients will generate different characteristics for IDD and OOD, paving a promising path toward novelty detection.

To compute the presence of the ODD data, it is necessary to test whether the gradient of a given data point is within the manifold of IDD. One approach is to use the Euclidean distances between a specific data point and the centers of each IDD. However the Euclidean distance is too sensitive to the variance of the gradients. This is due to the fact that given a pre-trained DNN, its weights are not always equally important to the final class decisions. Those which are of less importance to a particular class may experience gradients with more random magnitudes and directions, leading to a larger deviation. Therefore even for the IDD, we may observe large deviations in a certain variate of the gradient. To solve this issue, we adopt the Mahalanobis distance [14], which is computed similarly to the Euclidean distance, but with the inclusion of the covariance of the multi-variate distribution of the gradient of the IDD. The Mahalanobis distance metric has proved successful in many machine learning researchs such as [12,17,21,22]. Similar to [12] which defines the Mahalanaobis distance in the feature space, we define the gradient space Mahalanobis distance as:

$$M_x = (\nabla_c f(x) - \hat{\mu}_c)^T \hat{\Sigma}^{-1} (\nabla_c f(x) - \hat{\mu}_c) \tag{1}$$

where $\hat{\mu}_c$ is the gradient mean of the in-distribution samples $\mathcal{X}_{in}$ of the class c and $\hat{\Sigma}^{-1}$ is the tied precision matrix of all the known(training) classes. We use the equations below to estimate these two parameters:

$$\hat{\mu}_c = \frac{1}{N_c} \sum_{i:y_i=c} \nabla_c f(x_i^{in}) \tag{2}$$

$$\hat{\Sigma} = \frac{1}{N} \sum_c \sum_{i:y_i=c} (\nabla_c f(x_i^{in}) - \hat{\mu}_c)(\nabla_c f(x_i^{in}) - \hat{\mu}_c)^\top \tag{3}$$

where N_c is the amount of the IDD samples in the class c, N is the amount of the entire IDD training dataset.

We use Eqs. (2) and (3) to characterize the gradient distribution of the IDD by using the same training dataset of the DNN. After this class-specific distributions

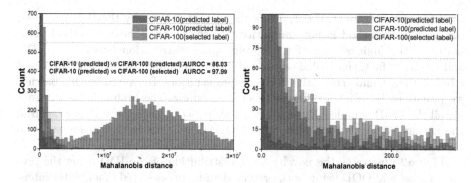

Fig. 2. (Left) The distribution of the Mahalanobis distance of in-distribution data using predicted label (highlighted in red), and OOD using both predicted label (highlighted in blue) and selected label (highlighted in green). (Right) The zoomed-in picture to the rectangle area of the left figure. By using the selected label for all the outliers, their novelty score distribution shifts away farther away from blue to green, as shown in the left figure, with less overlap with IDD data (the red distribution, as shown on the right.) (Color figure online)

estimation is done, we use Eq. (1) to measure how the gradient of the new input deviates from these estimated distributions.

In Eq. (1), $\nabla_c f(x)$ is the back-propagated gradient with respect to the class c. This raises a question of how to calculate the gradient of the OOD input since their ground-truth label Y_{ood} is not in the IDD label space $\mathcal{Y}_{in}$. To solve this problem, we propose to use the predicted label $Y_{ood}^{Pred} \in \mathcal{Y}_{in}$ to calculate and cross-entropy loss $\mathcal{L}(Y_{ood}^{Pred}; X_{ood}; \Theta)$ and do the back-propagation. From the manifold perspective, this means that we select the manifold closest to the input sample. This manifold requires the minimal amount of adaptation to the new input, i.e., the minimal gradient and Mahalanobis distance. If such Mahalanobis distance is still large, the input sample has a high probability to be an outlier.

Table 1. Comparison of AUROC results between the state-of-the-art [12,20] and our proposed novelty detector. The middle column is the performance of our novelty detector using the predicted label from the DNN for IDD to calculate the loss, gradients and Mahalanobis distance. The right column shows the performance boosting if we intentionally select the label to maximize the distance between IDD and OOD.

IDD (CIFAR-10)	AUROC		
OOD	State-of-the-art	Ours (with predicted label)	Ours (with selected label)
TinyImageNet	99.50	91.10	**99.92**
SVHN	99.90	91.63	**99.99**
LSUN	99.70	90.08	**99.99**
CIFAR-100	93.40	86.03	**97.99**

As shown in Table 1, if only using the predicted label by the IDD classifier, our proposed method is not competitive to the state-of-the-art method. This is due to the high overlap of the novelty score distribution between the IDD and OOD. In fact, the Mahalanobis distance is minimal if we use the predicted label as the ground truth label for back-propagation. To overcome this barrier, we intentionally select a different label to maximize the Mahalanobis distance for all the OOD samples. By doing that, we expect to achieve a larger mean of the novelty score distribution for the OOD. Consequently, it will be easier to threshold these OOD samples to reach higher detection accuracy.

Figure 2 illustrates the novelty score distribution of the IDD using the predicted label and OOD using both predicted and a pre-selected label. After intentionally using the selected label for all the OOD samples, the corresponding score distributions shift away from the in-distribution and thus, significantly improves the AUROC result (Table 1, Column 3). However, this raises a new problem: how to trigger the usage of different labels for IDD and OOD (i.e., predicted by the IDD classifier and the selected label, respectively), in the calculation of gradients? Here we introduce a binary classifier to pre-screen the input and make the initial IDD/OOD prediction. Based on the prediction result, our novelty detector chooses different label for gradient calculation.

Label Selection: To select a label Y^{Opt} that gives the maximum gradient distance, we propose to use the predicted softmax class probability:

$$Y^{Opt} = \operatorname*{argmin}_c(\sum_i Softmax(f(x_i^{ood}; \Theta))) \tag{4}$$

We use Eq. (4) to select the class that has the minimal average softmax probability for a batch of OOD data. This is equivalent to finding the least likely class for an OOD data to fall into. By using Y^{Opt}, its cross-entropy loss $\mathcal{L}(Y^{Opt}; X_{ood}; \Theta)$ becomes the maximum which results in the largest gradient and Mahalanobis distance. The only question left is where to find the OOD samples to estimate this label. We will address this issue in Subsect. 3.2.

3.2   Self-supervised Binary Classifier

To guide our novelty detector to use either the predicted or selected label in case of in-distribution or OOD input, we introduce a simple self-supervised binary classifier to screen IDD and OOD. The output from this binary classifier will be used to guide label selection in the pre-trained IDD classifier for gradient generation:

- For the predicted IDD input, the pre-trained model uses the predicted label Y^{Pred} for back-propagation.
- For the predicted OOD input, the model uses the selected label Y^{Opt}.

Unsupervised Preparation of OOD Samples for Initial Training: One key feature of our proposed method is to be self-supervised, which means no

OOD sample is available in advance. Therefore to create a dataset for the training of the binary classifier, we utilize the predicted IDD/OOD samples selected by the gradient-based novelty detector. For example, assuming the binary classifier is randomly initialized and a batch X^1 mixed with IDD and OOD data comes in, our novelty detector will first calculate the novelty confidence score $S^1 = \{s_1, s_2, ..., s_N\}_1$ using the predicted label. We select N/2 samples that correspond to the highest and lowest confidence scores in the S^1 as the binary classifier training data set $X^{pred} = \{X_{in}^{pred}, X_{ood}^{pred}\}$. This step helps select the best possible in-distribution and OOD data from the current batch so that the binary classifier's training inputs are reasonable. We use the X_{ood}^{pred} to select the label and use the X^{pred} to train the binary classifier. Once training is done, the following input batches will involve the cooperation from both the gradient-based novelty detector and the binary classifier.

3.3 Mutual Assistance Between the Binary Classifier and the Mahalanobis Path

The entire system is continuously exposed to a stream of unlabeled mini batch $X^1, X^2,...,$ where each X^i consists of N samples $\{x_1, x_2, ..., x_N\}$ mixed with IDD and OOD data. Due to the small size of the first batch X^1 and the relatively low performance of the novelty detector using the predicted label, the initial training of the binary classifier could not guarantee to be success. Therefore, an enhanced training (Fig. 1 and Algorithm 1) is required when more data is available. The training routine consists of three major steps: (1) Initial prediction of the binary classifier; (2) Calculation of the Mahalanobis score; and (3) Re-training of the binary classifier.

Initial Prediction of the Binary Classifier: When the new batch $X^k = \{x_1, x_2, ..., x_N\}_k$ arrives, the system first concatenates this new batch X^k with all the previously stored batches $X^{k-1}...X^1$. Given this concatenated batch, the binary classifier makes its initial outlier prediction $\{y_1', y_2', ..., y_{N \times k}' | y_i' \in (0, 1)\}$.

Calculation of the Mahalanobis Score: The gradient-based novelty detector takes the prediction result from the binary classifier and the concatenated batch. For each sample x_i in batch, our novelty detector first classifies it to one of the in-distribution class $y_i^{Pred} \in \mathcal{Y}_{in}$, then checks the binary classifier prediction y_i'. If y_i' is 0 (predicted in-distribution), use y_i^{Pred} as the ground truth label in the loss function for back-propagation, otherwise, use the pre-selected label y^{Opt}. After the gradient is available, we calculate the Mahalanobis distance s_i as the novelty confident score.

Re-training of the Binary Classifier: Given novelty confident score $S^k = \{s_1, s_2, ..., s_{N \times k}\}$ from the gradient-based novelty detector, we select $(N \times k)/2$ samples from the concatenated batch that correspond to the highest and lowest

---

Algorithm 1. Gradient-based Novelty Detection Boosted by Self-supervised Binary Classification

---

Input: In-distribution gradient distributions $\{\hat{\mu}, \hat{\Sigma}^{-1}\}$, batches for testing $[X^1, X^2, ..., X^k]$

1: **function** $noveltyScore$ $(X, \hat{\mu}, \hat{\Sigma}^{-1}, \hat{Y}, selected\_label)$
2:     $Mahalanobis\_Distance = list()$
3:     **for each** x in X **do**
4:         $c = None$ $//Label$ for $back\text{-}propagation$
5:         **if** Binary Classifier predict x as IDD **then**
6:             $c =$ Novelty detector predicted label
7:         **else**
8:             $c = selected\_label$
9:         **end if**
10:         $Score = (\nabla_c f(x) - \hat{\mu}_c)^T \hat{\Sigma}^{-1} (\nabla_c f(x) - \hat{\mu}_c)$
11:         $Mahalanobis\_Distance.append(Score)$
12:     **end for**
13:     **return** $Mahalanobis\_Distance$
14: **end function**
15: $X^{all} = None$
16: **while** new batch X^k is available **do**
17:     $X^{all} = X^{all} + X^k$ $//batch$ $concatenation$
18:     **if** X^k is the first batch **then**
19:         $S^{all} = noveltyScore(X^{all}, \hat{\mu}, \hat{\Sigma}^{-1})$
20:     **else**
21:         $\hat{Y} = binary$ $classifier$ $prediction$ on X^{all}
22:         $S^{all} = noveltyScore(X^{all}, \hat{\mu}, \hat{\Sigma}^{-1}, \hat{Y}, selected\_label)$
23:     **end if**
24:     Based on S^{all}, select samples from X^{all}
25: with the highest/lowest score as predicted X_{in}/X_{ood}
26:     Use X_{in}, X_{ood} to train binary classifier
27:     **if** $selected\_label$ is $None$ **then**
28:         $selected\_label = \underset{c}{\arg\min}(\sum_i Softmax(f(x_i^{ood})))$
29:     **end if**
30: **end while**
31: **return** $X_i \in X_{all}$ is an outliner if $S_i^{all} > threshold$

---

scores in S^k as a new training dataset for the binary classifier. Before training, we re-initialize the binary classifier to make sure the previous model will not be inherited into the current stage. Once training is done, our system is updated with the knowledge of all previous batches and is ready to process next available inputs with higher detection accuracy.

As shown in Fig. 1, this mutual assistance continues with more unlabelled data, which keeps improving the accuracy of both the unsupervised detection engine and the binary classifier. These two units help each other in this closed loop.

4 Experiments and Results

4.1 Experimental Setup

We use three pre-trained ResNet-34 networks [6] provided by [12] as the base of our gradient-based novelty detector. Each model is trained on CIFAR-10, CIFAR-100 [9] and SVHN [15] with the testing accuracy of 93.67%, 78.34% and 96.68% accordingly. To calculate the gradient-based Mahalanobis distance, we only use the gradient extracted from the last layer of the feature extractor. Our simple binary classifier has the structure of three convolution layers and one batch normalization layer with a Sigmoid classifier. It is trained by minimizing the cross-entropy loss using Adam [8]. The initial learning rate is set to 0.0002 and the decay rate is controlled by $\beta_1 = 0.5$ and $\beta_2 = 0.999$. We train it for 500 epochs in both initial training and re-training process. Regarding the batch size, we find that the amount of IDD and OOD samples in each batch, and the batch size itself have a strong impact on the performance of the binary classifier and the overall system, as discussed in Subsect. 4.2.

Our experiment includes three in-distribution datasets: CIFAR-10, CIFAR-100 and SVHN. We test each of them using the other two as the OOD. In addition, we use two more OOD datasets: the resized version of the ImageNet [18] and LSUN [23] provided by [13]. Each of these two datasets contains 10,000 images with size 32 by 32. For all three in-distribution datasets, we use only the testing portion of the images because the training portion has already been used to train the novelty detector. For each IDD/OOD pair, we randomly select 5,000/5,000 (IDD/OOD) as the training dataset and further divide them into mini batches with size of 100/100 (IDD/OOD) to emulate the data streaming, the rest 5,000/5,000 (IDD/OOD) samples are used to test the binary classifier accuracy and the overall novelty detection performance after each new batch has been taken into the system. We evaluate our detector with two performance metrics: AUROC and AUPR. All experiments are performed with PyTorch [16] on one NVIDIA GeForce RTX 2080 platform.

4.2 Batch Training of the Binary Classifier

Inspired from the discriminator in the GAN [4] that can successfully distinguish the real images from the fake ones, we use the similar discriminator loss in our binary classifier training, where the loss from the IDD and OOD data are calculated separately. During the prediction phase, the binary classifier achieves high accuracy if the input batch contains either in-distribution or OOD samples. This is because the batch norm layer averages the difference within each group of data (i.e., IDD or OOD) while stressing the difference between IDD and OOD inputs. For each novelty detection experiment, we adopt this batch-based approach and present the results of using different batch size where each batch contains only IDD or OOD data.

Table 2. Comprehensive evaluation of AUROC on multiple IDD and OOD benchmarks.

Dataset		AUROC						
IDD	OOD	Ours (Batch = 8)	Ours (Batch = 32)	Ours (Batch = 128)	SSD[a]	Mahalanobis[b] (feature based)	Confounding label[c]	ODIN[d]
4*CIFAR-10	TinyImageNet	99.90	**99.92**	99.85	-	99.5	93.18	98.5
	CIFAR-100	84.79	93.51	**97.99**	94.0	-	-	-
	LSUN	**99.99**	99.97	**99.99**	-	99.7	99.86	99.2
	SVHN	99.94	**99.99**	**99.99**	99.9	99.1	99.84	-
4*CIFAR-100	TinyImageNet	**99.49**	99.28	99.28	-	98.2	-	85.5
	CIFAR-10	72.61	89.76	**91.38**	84.0	-	-	-
	LSUN	99.57	**99.59**	99.55	-	98.2	-	86.0
	SVHN	99.79	99.79	**99.82**	99.5	98.4	-	-
4*SVHN	CIFAR-10	99.94	**99.96**	99.95	-	99.3	99.79	-
	TinyImageNet	99.95	**99.97**	99.95	-	99.9	99.77	-
	LSUN	99.96	99.97	**99.98**	-	99.9	99.93	-
	CIFAR-100	99.65	99.74	**99.78**	-	-	-	-

[a][20].[b][12].[c][11].[d][13].

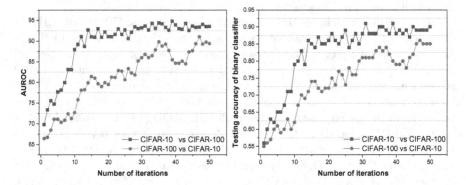

Fig. 3. AUROC in our novelty detector (Left) and the testing accuracy of the binary classifier (Right) during the mutual assistance (i.e., number of iterations). Each point corresponds to the moment when a new batch arrives into the system. As the accuracy of the binary classifier increases, the novelty detector receives more boosting.

4.3   Performance Evaluation of Novelty Detection

Table 2 presents the performance of our proposed method as compared to other novelty detectors. Our method outperforms all previous supervised and unsupervised works across all IDD/OOD setup. In particular, our method improves the AUROC of the experiment where CIFAR100 as IDD and CIFAR10 as OOD by up to ∼5 and ∼7 with batch size 32 and 128 accordingly. These two datasets are very similar to each other. Therefore it's extremely challenging to detect the outlier in previous approaches. With the new framework, our method significantly improves the state-of-the-art.

Figure 3 illustrates the stepwise improvement of our framework. Each point in the curve corresponds to the intermediate testing accuracy of the binary classifier and the AUROC of the system after every new batch of unlabelled data (100/100) arrives. From the curves, we can observe the efficacy of mutual assistance between the binary classifier and the novelty detector. The initial testing accuracy of the binary classifier reaches around 90 in all three IDD/OOD experiments, which proves that our self-supervised approach based on the novelty detector's output is effective. As more data is received, every re-training on the binary classifier improves its accuracy, contributed by increasingly higher confidence of the IDD/OOD prediction from the novelty detector. In turn, the novelty detector's performance is boosted, benefiting from higher accuracy of the binary classifier and better label selection. Such positive feedback eventually drives the performance of the overall framework, reaching high accuracy of both the novelty detector and the binary classifier.

4.4 One-Class Learning with the OOD Detector

We further apply our OOD detector to one-class learning, using CIFAR-10 as the example. In this case, we first train the ResNet-34 network with nine classes (IDD) together and then consider the last tenth class as the new learning task (OOD). Our goal is to detect and learn the OOD class without triggering the catastrophic forgetting on the previous learned IDD classes. Different from previous experimental setup where an equal amount of IDD/OOD samples (5,000/5,000) are used, we attempt to minimize the amount of IDD samples (i.e., 500 and 1,000 in our experiments) to emulate the memory rehearsal. We still allow more OOD samples (4,000) streaming into the system.

Unlike novelty detection where the output is binary (IDD or OOD), the continual learning problem requires the system to predict a label across all known IDD classes plus the new OOD class, i.e., single-head classification. Since the binary classifier is already trained to distinguish between IDD and OOD during the novelty detection procedure, we can further utilize it as an add-on to the primary neural network for classifying the OOD samples. To merge this binary classifier into our main model for continual learning purpose, we test two frameworks: (1) the parallel structure where the concatenated features from both the primary novelty detector and binary classifier are sent to a merged fully-connected layer and (2) a sequential structure where the binary classifier makes initial IDD/OOD prediction. Then the predicted IDDs are sent to the primary neural network for IDD classification, as shown in Fig. 4.

The Parallel Structure with Merged FC Layer: As shown in Fig. 4 (Left), we use both the binary classifier and primary neural network as two feature extractors for the same input and send the concatenated output features to a single fully-connected (FC) layer. The output dimension of this FC layer is the number of IDD classes plus one, which corresponds to the newly learned OOD class. We use the IDD and OOD samples that are available during the novelty detection phase to train this FC layer and all the rest parameters in both two models are fixed.

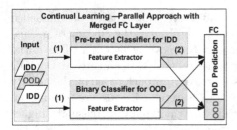 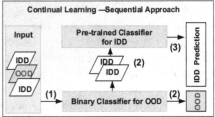

Fig. 4. The merged parallel structure (Left) and the sequential structure (Right) for one-class continual learning. **The merged parallel approach**: (1) Samples are sent to both the primary neural network and the binary classifier. (2) The extracted features from two models are concatenated and sent to the fully-connected (FC) layer for label prediction. **The sequential approach**: (1) Samples are sent to the binary classifier for IDD/OOD prediction. (2) The predicted IDD samples from the binary classifier are sent to the downstream pre-trained IDD classifier. The predicted OOD samples are classified as the new class. (3) The IDD classifier makes IDD class prediction.

Table 3. The classification accuracy tested on each class of CIFAR-10 in one-class continual learning using the parallel structure. For each row in this table, nine classes are first learned together and the tenth class (as shown in the first column of the table) is learned through our proposed framework.

OOD	Airplane	Auto	Bird	Cat	Deer	Dog	Frog	Horse	Ship	Truck	Single-head Acc
Airplane	93.3	88.7	97.2	89.9	88.1	95.5	89.2	95.7	95.2	92.9	92.6
Auto	93.6	84.7	93.0	91.8	87.1	95.4	92.3	96.0	95.5	94.6	92.4
Bird	91.6	97.3	96.6	80.1	78.6	90.0	85.4	90.8	93.0	94.0	89.8
Cat	93.7	95.8	91.1	96.5	80.0	92.1	69.8	94.7	93.9	96.1	90.4
Deer	92.3	97.2	84.3	79.7	94.1	85.4	83.3	91.2	90.7	95.6	89.4
Dog	93.7	95.7	87.8	61.8	94.2	96.0	86.5	95.2	92.4	95.7	90.0
Frog	95.5	96.6	82.9	83.1	91.8	89.9	95.8	88.4	94.7	95.6	91.4
Horse	95.6	96.4	91.0	82.2	88.5	84.9	95.4	96.5	86.4	95.8	91.3
Ship	87.6	97.3	93.9	86.8	95.3	90.7	95.4	95.6	91.4	85.6	92.0
Truck	93.5	86.7	92.5	88.3	95.9	90.8	96.7	96.1	93.4	91.1	92.5
Average	93.0	93.6	91.0	84.0	89.4	82.1	89.0	94.0	92.7	93.7	91.2
Baseline	95.8	98.1	92.1	88.3	95.1	90.3	96.3	95.9	96.1	96.8	94.5

To test this framework, we conduct ten experiments considering each class from CIFAR-10 dataset as the OOD and randomly select 1,000 samples from the remaining nine classes as the IDD. We first conduct the novelty detection procedure proposed in the previous section and then merge the trained binary classifier and primary neural network with a 10-class FC layer. Table 3 shows the testing accuracy of our framework. Each row corresponds to an experiment considering one class as OOD and each column corresponds to the testing accuracy for a particular class. To compare our performance with the baseline, we

Table 4. The classification accuracy tested on each class of CIFAR-10 in one-class continual learning using the sequential structure. For each row in this table, nine classes are first learned together and the tenth class (as shown in the first column of the table) is learned through our proposed framework.

OOD	Airplane	Auto	Bird	Cat	Deer	Dog	Frog	Horse	Ship	Truck	Single-head Acc
Airplane	93.7	98.2	95.6	89.8	97.2	92.6	96.9	96.8	98.6	96.5	94.9
Auto	96.7	85.1	93.3	89.0	95.6	94.2	97.8	96.4	97.1	97.8	92.4
Bird	99.1	98.9	78.9	94.4	97.9	95.7	98.6	98.4	98.2	98.4	89.4
Cat	96.8	97.7	93.8	90.4	96.8	96.2	97.6	97.1	97.1	97.9	94.6
Deer	96.3	97.1	93.9	89.5	97.9	91.8	97.0	98.4	97.5	97.2	96.1
Dog	95.8	98.0	94.6	94.0	96.9	93.1	97.7	97.1	97.6	96.3	95.4
Frog	96.4	98.4	93.2	91.8	96.3	91.9	99.2	97.2	96.5	96.8	96.4
Horse	96.6	97.7	93.0	88.0	97.3	93.1	97.7	85.6	97.0	95.5	92.4
Ship	97.7	98.3	94.9	88.3	96.5	91.2	96.7	96.9	99.4	97.2	96.4
Truck	95.5	99.3	94.0	91.7	96.9	93.2	97.2	96.0	97.8	74.6	89.4
Average	96.5	96.9	92.5	90.7	96.9	93.3	97.6	96.0	97.7	94.8	93.7
Baseline	95.8	98.1	92.1	88.3	95.1	90.3	96.3	95.9	96.1	96.8	94.5

train a ResNet-34 using all ten classes and report the class-wise testing accuracy in the last row. We find that by using this parallel structure, the testing accuracy are dropped by 1–5% compared with the baseline accuracy, which means the features extracted from the binary classifier are partially correlated to those from the main neural network, resulting in performance degradation.

The Sequential Structure with Separated FC Layer: As shown in Fig. 4 (Right), we give the priority to the binary classifier and employ it to make the initial IDD/OOD prediction. Those samples that are predicted as IDD are then sent to the downstream pre-trained IDD classifier to recognize the belonging to those IDD classes. Therefore, this procedure completes one-class continual learning where the classification for OOD class is completed by the single binary classifier and the remaining IDD classes are handled by the main neural network. Compared with the previous parallel structure, this one does not require any re-training of the FC layer. The primary neural network is untouched and thus, their baseline accuracy on IDD class is preserved.

Similar to the testing procedure that conducted on the parallel structure, we conduct the same experiment on this sequential structure and Table 4 shows its performance. Both the class-wise and single-head testing accuracy are closed to their baseline performance which proves its success over the parallel structure. The high performance benefits from the fact that both the binary classifier and the primary neural network are left untouched thus each individual part is working at its best without the interference from the other part. This structure completely avoid triggering the catastrophic forgetting on the IDD classes since there is no re-training required on the IDD classifier. Compared with [3] which used memory budget of 2,000 IDD samples with the accuracy <90%, our proposed method achieves 89–96% accuracy in any class with only 1,000 IDD samples.

5   Conclusion

In this paper, we propose a new framework for novelty detection, which involves the cooperation of a gradient-based novelty detector and a self-supervised binary classifier. We first introduce the Mahalanobis distance in the gradient space as a novelty measure metric and discuss the impact of label selection on the novelty score. We then introduce a binary classifier to guide label selection and develop a self-supervised training solution. With mutually assistance between these two components, our proposed framework outperforms previous supervised and unsupervised approaches in all benchmarks. For instance, our method achieves superior performance on CIFAR-100 vs. CIFAR-10 case by improving AUROC from 84% to 91% compared with the state-of-the-art.

In addition, we propose the parallel and sequential frameworks for one-class continual learning that utilizes the product from our proposed novelty detection procedure. We prove that the binary classifier is well capable of detecting the OOD samples and thus, placing it next to the primary neural network as an add-on benefits learning the new OOD class. Our proposed sequential framework achieves the state-of-the-art single-head accuracy with only 1,000 memory budget.

Acknowledgements. This research was supported in part by the U.S. Department of Energy, through the Office of Advanced Scientific Computing Research's "Data-Driven Decision Control for Complex Systems (DnC2S)" project. It was also partially supported by C-BRIC, one of six centers in JUMP, a Semiconductor Research Corporation (SRC) program sponsored by DARPA. Pacific Northwest National Laboratory is operated by Battelle Memorial Institute for the U.S. Department of Energy under Contract No. DE-AC05-76RL01830. Oak Ridge National Laboratory is operated by UT-Battelle LLC for the U.S. Department of Energy under contract number DE-AC05-00OR22725.

References

1. Abati, D., Porrello, A., Calderara, S., Cucchiara, R.: Latent space autoregression for novelty detection. In: Proceedings of the IEEE/CVF Conference on Computer Vision and Pattern Recognition, pp. 481–490 (2019)
2. Chen, J., Sathe, S., Aggarwal, C., Turaga, D.: Outlier detection with autoencoder ensembles. In: Proceedings of the 2017 SIAM International Conference on Data Mining, pp. 90–98. SIAM (2017)
3. Du, X., Li, Z., Seo, J.s., Liu, F., Cao, Y.: Noise-based selection of robust inherited model for accurate continual learning. In: Proceedings of the IEEE/CVF Conference on Computer Vision and Pattern Recognition Workshops, pp. 244–245 (2020)
4. Goodfellow, I.J., et al.: Generative adversarial networks. arXiv preprint arXiv:1406.2661 (2014)

5. Hawkins, S., He, H., Williams, G., Baxter, R.: Outlier detection using replicator neural networks. In: Kambayashi, Y., Winiwarter, W., Arikawa, M. (eds.) DaWaK 2002. LNCS, vol. 2454, pp. 170–180. Springer, Heidelberg (2002). https://doi.org/10.1007/3-540-46145-0_17
6. He, K., Zhang, X., Ren, S., Sun, J.: Deep residual learning for image recognition. In: Proceedings of the IEEE Conference on Computer Vision and Pattern Recognition, pp. 770–778 (2016)
7. Hendrycks, D., Gimpel, K.: A baseline for detecting misclassified and out-of-distribution examples in neural networks. arXiv preprint arXiv:1610.02136 (2016)
8. Kingma, D.P., Ba, J.: Adam: A method for stochastic optimization. arXiv preprint arXiv:1412.6980 (2014)
9. Krizhevsky, A., et al.: Learning multiple layers of features from tiny images (2009)
10. Kwon, G., Prabhushankar, M., Temel, D., AlRegib, G.: Novelty detection through model-based characterization of neural networks. In: 2020 IEEE International Conference on Image Processing (ICIP), pp. 3179–3183. IEEE (2020)
11. Lee, J., AlRegib, G.: Gradients as a measure of uncertainty in neural networks. In: 2020 IEEE International Conference on Image Processing (ICIP), pp. 2416–2420. IEEE (2020)
12. Lee, K., Lee, K., Lee, H., Shin, J.: A simple unified framework for detecting out-of-distribution samples and adversarial attacks. arXiv preprint arXiv:1807.03888 (2018)
13. Liang, S., Li, Y., Srikant, R.: Enhancing the reliability of out-of-distribution image detection in neural networks. arXiv preprint arXiv:1706.02690 (2017)
14. Mahalanobis, P.C.: On the generalized distance in statistics. Proc. Natl. Inst. Sci. **2**, 49–55 (1936)
15. Netzer, Y., Wang, T., Coates, A., Bissacco, A., Wu, B., Ng, A.Y.: Reading digits in natural images with unsupervised feature learning (2011)
16. Paszke, A., et al.: Automatic differentiation in pytorch (2017)
17. Roth, P.M., Hirzer, M., Köstinger, M., Beleznai, C., Bischof, H.: Mahalanobis distance learning for person re-identification. In: Gong, S., Cristani, M., Yan, S., Loy, C.C. (eds.) Person Re-Identification. ACVPR, pp. 247–267. Springer, London (2014). https://doi.org/10.1007/978-1-4471-6296-4_12
18. Russakovsky, O., et al.: ImageNet large scale visual recognition challenge. Int. J. Comput. Vision **115**(3), 211–252 (2015). https://doi.org/10.1007/s11263-015-0816-y
19. Sakurada, M., Yairi, T.: Anomaly detection using autoencoders with nonlinear dimensionality reduction. In: Proceedings of the MLSDA 2014 2nd Workshop on Machine Learning for Sensory Data Analysis, pp. 4–11 (2014)
20. Sehwag, V., Chiang, M., Mittal, P.: SSD: a unified framework for self-supervised outlier detection. arXiv preprint arXiv:2103.12051 (2021)
21. Shen, C., Kim, J., Wang, L.: Scalable large-margin mahalanobis distance metric learning. IEEE Trans. Neural Netw. **21**(9), 1524–1530 (2010)
22. Xiang, S., Nie, F., Zhang, C.: Learning a mahalanobis distance metric for data clustering and classification. Pattern Recogn. **41**(12), 3600–3612 (2008)
23. Yu, F., Seff, A., Zhang, Y., Song, S., Funkhouser, T., Xiao, J.: LSUN: construction of a large-scale image dataset using deep learning with humans in the loop (2016)
24. Zhou, C., Paffenroth, R.C.: Anomaly detection with robust deep autoencoders. In: Proceedings of the 23rd ACM SIGKDD International Conference on Knowledge Discovery and Data Mining, pp. 665–674 (2017)

Author Index

Printed in the United States
by Baker & Taylor Publisher Services

Printed in the United States
by Baker & Taylor Publisher Services